POLITICAL PLATONISM

ALEXANDER DUGIN

POLITICAL PLATONISM

THE PHILISOPHY OF POLITICS

ARKTOS
LONDON 2019

ΛRKTOS

⊕ Arktos.com 😃 fb.com/Arktos ◐ @arktosmedia ◎ arktosmedia

ISBN
978-1-917646-17-8 (Paperback)
978-1-917646-18-5 (Ebook)

Translation & Editing
Michael Millerman
Ciarán Ó Conaill

Layout & Cover
Tor Westman

CONTENTS

1. **The Philosophy of Politics**   **1**

2. **Deconstruction of Democracy**   **11**

    The Concept of "Democracy" Is Not Neutral and Not Self-Evident   11

    Demos in "Democracy": Aristotle's Etymology   13

    The Metaphysical Foundations of Democracy:
      The Hypotheses of the *Parmenides*   15

    The Hypotheses of the *Parmenides* and Types of Democracy   16

    Political Platonism   19

3. **Political Platonism and Its Ontological Bases**   **23**

    Part 1. Total Homologies of Power in Platonism   23

    Part 2. The Structures of Platonopolis and
      the Hypotheses of the *Parmenides*   25

    Part 3. The Aristomorphosis of Politics in Aristotle   28

    Conclusion   29

4. **Traditionalism against Devilopolis**   **31**

    From Progress to Eschatology: A Change of Reference Points   31

    Traditionalism as Philosophy and Its Appearance in Russia   32

    René Guénon: The Foundations of Philosophy   34

    Julius Evola's *Revolt Against the Modern World*   38

    Traditionalism and Non-Conformism   39

    Reasons for the Relevance of Traditionalism   40

    Towards Political Platonism   42

    Critique of Devilopolis: Opening the "World Egg" from Below   43

    Russia's Eschatological Choice   45

5. Plato's Relevance for Russia and
    the Platonic Minimum   47

6. Christianity and Neo-Platonism   53

7. Heraclitus and Contemporary Russia   57

8. A Conversation about Noomachy   63

9. The Existential Theory of Society   87

    Implicit Sociology   87
    Volk Als Dasein   88
    The Existential Structure of the Volk   90
    The Project of Authentic Society: The Existential Empire 97
    The Narod and Its God: The Religion of Selbst   100

10. Thinking Chaos and the Other
    Beginning of Philosophy   103

1.

THE PHILOSOPHY
OF POLITICS

This is a transcript of the first thirty-five minutes of the first lecture of a course on "The Philosophy of Politics" that Dugin gave at Moscow State University in 2014. The entire lecture series is available in Russian on Dugin's Youtube Channel.

First, let us consider the nature of this discipline and what it studies. If we look at the history of philosophy and of political systems, we will see the following regularity. Philosophy and politics, from the very beginning, from the very birth of these two disciplines, developed not only in parallel, but inseparably from one another. Among the Seven Sages, considered the founders of the Greek Pre-Socratic philosophical tradition, there are many, including Solon, who are famous for writing political laws, constitutions, and criminal codes, and who were essentially political actors representing their cities, and their political units. So at the very beginning of the history of philosophy, we see an inseparable connection between philosophy and politics. Viewing politics as a separate phenomenon, disconnected from philosophy, is completely foreign to the origins of the philosophical tradition.

The philosophy of politics is deeper than this. It is a discipline that considers the philosophers who engage in politics, the philosophers who write about politics, and the political actors who base their laws, the establishment of their political system, on philosophical principles. The subject matter of philosophy and of politics is that originary sphere that unites philosophy and politics in a certain shared orientation. In other words, I want to say that we are not artificially uniting two spheres, one of politics, and one of philosophy, but are removing an artificial distinction. We do not study politics with the help of philosophy, and we are not speaking about the political philosophy of one or another school, period, culture, or civilization. When we speak of the philosophy of politics, we are talking about the essence of politics, of that which makes politics politics — on the one hand. On the other, we are talking about the political essence of philosophy, which makes philosophy philosophy.

There is a difference between the two, however. Philosophy predominates here, because politics without philosophy is not possible at all. Politics is a form of applied philosophy; it is the application of philosophy to a certain sphere of human life. Philosophy without politics, however, is possible, theoretically. That is, there is a philosophy that does not occupy itself with politics, but there is no politics that is not based on philosophy. So, there is an inequality here; philosophy predominates. Nevertheless, philosophy studies politics; not only the philosophical foundations thereof, but also the political aspects of philosophy itself; because politics is not a partial and accidental application of philosophy, but the most general, most fundamental, yet applied, element of philosophy. As soon as philosophy appears, it necessarily, first of all, when it exists, turns to politics; and all politics emerges from philosophy. Between them there exists an unequal, but very deep, organic connection. There, where this original unification of the philosophical and the political occurs, the birth of all possible political systems and at the same time the crystallization of philosophical knowledge happens.

Although there is a philosophy that, free from politics, occupies itself with non-political questions, even such a free, non-political philosophy is connected in one way or another with politics, inasmuch as philosophy and politics have a common root. For this reason, if philosophy considers aesthetic questions, historical questions, and cultural questions, and says nothing about politics, this does not mean that it is a completely separate phenomenon. Any philosophy at all, even the most abstract, has a political dimension, in some cases explicitly. In the case of Solon, as in the case of the ancient Greek Pre-Socratics and Sages, and as in the case of Plato and Aristotle, this is an explicit dimension of philosophy, but there is also an implicit political dimension of philosophy. When philosophy says nothing about politics, it still has the presence of a philosophical paradigm of one kind or another, which carries in itself the possibility of a political dimension. In one case it is explicit, open, and manifest; in the other, it is implicit and contained.

Because of this, there is a very deep connection between philosophy and politics, a connection at the level of their origin. The study of philosophy without politics already in itself impoverishes and weakens the concept of philosophy. On the other hand, the study of politics without philosophy is not at all valid. In that case, we've already gone the way of programming and established rule by [Microsoft] Word; that is, open file, close file. We are good programmers. ... We know two functions, save and save as. We can be excellent users of Word, we can write very good texts on Word, but we are not programmers. People who do not have the philosophy of politics, who do not have philosophy, they are as much politicians as computer programmers are. In fact, a person who does not know philosophy cannot engage in politics; he's not a politician. He is a hired government worker who is simply in front of a wall. Someone has told him: go there, do that. What to do, where to go. ... He might be an excellent user, but in reality politicians who lack a philosophical dimension are merely on a construction-site, some foreign construction-site. ... In reality, without philosophy, there is no politics, period. Politics is one of the dimensions contained within philosophy.

Politics without philosophy does not exist, but philosophy without politics does exist, because it is primary in relation to politics; but all philosophy has a political dimension — either, as I said, explicitly, or implicitly, in which case we are silent about it. This silence of philosophy concerning its political dimension or expression is not a total silence; it is more reticence than silence. That is, philosophy that does not occupy itself with politics knows about politics, and has it within itself, but openly does not speak about it. This is a peculiar silence. There is the silence of the wise man, and there is the silence of the fool. The fool stays silent in order not to say the wrong thing, because he senses that if he starts to talk, nothing good will come of it. The wise man stays silent for a completely different reason. The silence of philosophy concerning politics is the silence of the wise man, but, if we inquire of the wise man properly, he will tell us what he knows about politics and what he tells will be entirely sensible. He is, however, silent.

So, any philosophical system carries in itself a political dimension, but not every philosophical system develops this model explicitly. That's the most important thing in order to understand the sphere of the subject matter that we will be studying in the course of the philosophy of politics. In other words, we are studying the philosophical root, the base, the programming base, and the matrix base, of all politics, which is entirely reducible to philosophy — there is nothing in politics, not a single element, which does not lead to, is not explained by, and does not emerge from philosophy. Simply, politics is a part of philosophy,

so we'll be studying that. We'll also be studying the political dimension of philosophy; on the other hand, the philosophy which carries
politics within it is of course richer than politics, but nevertheless in
any philosophical system we can discover, even there where nothing is
said about it, a possible application to the political sphere, i.e. the possibility of deriving from philosophy political content. […] Politics is if
you will the most important case of the application of philosophy. […]

Accordingly, the history of philosophy and the history of politics
produce strictly one and the same pattern. This is extremely important. There exists a precise homology between them. If philosophy
moves in one direction, politics cannot move in another direction.
Politics moves together with philosophy. If something has changed in
philosophy, something will change in politics. If something changed in
politics, something changed in philosophy, which predetermined this
change in politics. Politics has no autonomy from philosophy. Politics
is often more visible, though sometimes less so. From the perspective of history, the changes of dynasties, of a certain leader, prince,
imperator … [the decision] to start a war … this is evident, this is a
political decision, but it is never distinct from philosophy. It is what
we see — the political decision — but we do not see the philosophical
decision, which must be there. From the perspective of the philosophy
of politics, political history is a section of the history of philosophy,
depending on this philosophical history absolutely. No politician is
free from philosophy, and no philosopher can fail to be viewed in the
light of his implicit political dimension. In other words, the historical picture, history, history as such, the rise and fall of kingdoms, the
construction and death of civilizations, conflicts between civilizations,
political revolutions … decisions about tramways … all this has a
philosophical dimension behind it, not always evident and not always
recognized, but the task of those who study the philosophy of politics
is to elaborate the entirety of this total homology, this equal (homo)

meaning (Logos). The meaning of history is political-philosophical or philosophical-political. All history has these two sides. On the one hand it is the history of kingdoms, on the other it is the history of ideas. The history of kingdoms and the history of ideas are not separate; it is one and the same history. Thus, if we fasten onto the philosophical dimension, for instance the transition from subjective idealism to objective idealism, this is necessarily connected with an identical political dimension, a transition from one political model to another, changes in the configurations of religions — and this is a philosophical problem in the first place, theology — radical changes in the content of the political processes occurring in the society where this philosophy is spreading. We can approach this homology between the philosophical and the political from all sides. We can say the political system changed, and we can specify the direction, speed, and content of the change. We can, even if we know nothing of the philosophy of that period, establish what was going on on the level of philosophical issues.

Or the opposite: we don't know what happened politically in some society, but the history of the arguments of one philosopher with another was preserved; from this history of arguments, if it is written down correctly, we can reconstruct the whole political picture of what was happening in that moment, in the agora where everything was decided democratically, in the ding or the veche, or if there was a monarchy, theocracy, or an empire. In other words, to study the philosophy of politics, we begin with a certain axiom, the axiom of the absolute homology between the political and the philosophical.

Of course we can make a certain distinction between politics and the political. I want to draw attention to one of the most eminent philosophers of politics, Carl Schmitt; we will refer to him throughout the entire course. In the 21st century, it is commonly agreed that Carl Schmitt was the most outstanding political philosopher of the 20th century. At some times this was doubted; it was said that there are other philosophers ... but today if you say "Carl Schmitt," everywhere you'll be told that he is one of the most outstanding political philosophers; maybe the most outstanding, alongside Hobbes and alongside Plato. That is, Carl Schmitt is the political philosopher par excellence. I want to draw your attention to his works, and recommend that everyone necessarily and without delay familiarize themselves with his work on the political, *das Politische*. This is very important. Carl Schmitt distinguishes politics and the Political. He considers the Political — written with a capital P — in this case it is an adjective considered as a noun: *das* is the article indicating that we are talking about a noun. In German this is very clear: *das Politische*, as opposed to mere *politische*. In order to convey Schmitt's meaning, we use the capital letter, the Political [henceforth, I will not capitalize; it is necessary in Russian, where there is no definite article.] This — the political — Schmitt distinguishes from politics. By politics, he understands the application of the political to a concrete social situation. The concretization of politics is the concretization of the political, but what, then, is the political? The political — *das Politische* — is precisely that point where the son (politics) is connected with the father (philosophy). That is, the political is precisely the sphere of philosophical politics, the sphere where philosophy connects directly with politics, what we called the homology of philosophy and politics. In other words, *das Politische*, according to Schmitt, is precisely the point of homology where we speak not of politics ... but not yet of philosophy at a broader level. It is the border, the horizon, the line between philosophy and politics. That is what *das Politische* means.

Another interesting aspect is that it is a certain sphere, a sphere that we define precisely as the philosophy of politics. The entire sphere of the philosophy of politics is contained in this concept of the political, *das Politische*.

Another very important concept Schmitt employs is what is called a "fore-concept" [*Vorgriffe*]. The fore-concept is not yet a political law, it is not yet a political institution, is a not a political party, nor is it a concrete political program. The fore-concept is a kind of element or singularity of the political in its pure guise — not purely philosophical, but where the philosophy of politics steps into its own right. Carl Schmitt calls this a fore-concept. The field of the political thus consists entirely of fore-concepts, political fore-concepts.

The political fore-concept is also a very interesting phenomenon in itself. It is precisely that moment of transition when philosophy becomes politics, but notice the tense: it becomes; it has not yet become, but only becomes. When philosophy becomes politics, we are dealing with a political concept. This is the political concept, for instance, of the separation of powers, the relation of Church and State, notions of borders, the subject, and political institutions. These are already political concepts, in the full sense of the word. When, then, is something a fore-concept? When the birth of a political concept is prepared on the basis of philosophical content. In this way, the sphere of the political is the sphere of the existence of fore-concepts. The political consists of fore-concepts; and studying fore-concepts, we study that homology about which we spoke earlier. The study of the homology of philosophy and politics, of what is common between these two asymmetrical spheres, is the study of fore-concepts and the task of the philosophy of politics. This is what we are talking about. We are talking about a kind of field that exists, where the multiplicity of the philosophical intersects with the multiplicity of politics. Here between them is precisely what is common: the political, which the philosophy of politics studies.

That was the introduction. Now we move to the question of how this occurs in practice. Plato is considered the founder of the first full-fledged philosophical system in history. He formulated most completely the philosophical agenda that predetermined the entire ancient history of philosophy, the entire Middle Ages, and to a significant extent the philosophy of the Renaissance, that anticipated the philosophy of Modernity. Moreover, there is not today, in the 21st century, a philosopher more relevant and less understood than Plato. In other words, Plato is all of philosophy [the whole of philosophy; philosophy *in toto*]. The sharpest thinkers of the 19th, 18th, 17th, 16th, 15th ... and so on until Plato all study Plato. In fact, strictly speaking there is one philosopher: Plato, and this is philosophy. To this day we have not [inaudible] his agenda. Concerning each of Plato's words, of each of his phrases, there are heated arguments to this day, and no one can ascertain fully whether that is the way he was understood. Geniuses arise to take one position; geniuses arise and oppose it. Not simple people. Philosophical geniuses. ... All Christian dogma is based on Plato. In Christian theology there is not one thesis that does not have a Platonic dimension. In Islamic theology, everything is based exclusively on Platonism, and even where Platonism did not reach, in India, nevertheless the simplest way to study Hindu philosophy, Vedas, religion, is with Platonism, because the analogy is at once obvious.

So, Plato is considered the prince of the philosophers, and no one has yet been able to attack his kingdom in philosophy. Thousands of times it was announced that Plato's empire has fallen. These proved each time to be some kind of marginal hallucinations. We live in the philosophy of Plato, Plato is the prince of philosophy, and either we contest this, in which case we imitate the rise of the slaves who try to break free from the might of Plato's kingdom, or else we simply accept it as loyal citizens and follow our Emperor, Plato.

The idea that philosophy has brought something supplementary to Plato is an entirely unfounded, unscientific academic hypothesis. It is a kind of rumor, which is not confirmed by the scientific community. Even those regarded as the embodiment of modern philosophy studied Plato. [Here, Dugin talks about Bergson, who gave us, through the "primitive and very limited" Karl Popper, the open society, and about Whitehead, to show that both, though modern, were inspired by Plato.] Plato is everything. In fact, if someone reads Plato, he comes up against not just one philosopher, not one author, not one school; he comes up against philosophy as such, because all philosophy is nothing other than the movement between a few of Plato's theses. Plato founded all philosophy at once: at once, and all together. The study of philosophy is the study of the philosophy of Plato. Everything else, essentially — as Whitehead, an analytical philosopher, a logician, a mathematician, himself said — is a footnote to the philosophy of Plato, so we must attend to the fact that philosophy is only Plato.

If we do not understand Plato, we do not understand the programming language of philosophy. […] The study of philosophy begins with the study of the works of Plato; the study of philosophy originates in the study of works of Plato; the study of philosophy ends with the study of the works of Plato; there's enough here for a lifetime. Accordingly, one can — I'll generalize here. This is a program for geniuses. For a simple, ordinary philosopher, it is possible to take one of Plato's dialogues. If I take the *Cratylus* [for instance], and live my life with the *Cratylus*, by the end of my life, the clarity of the *Cratylus* will be total. For students, the matter narrows. Let us take a separate saying of Plato and try, in the course of some extent of time, to live it through. Even that will be enormous, because Plato is philosophy. Accordingly, if we talk of philosophy, we talk of Plato. […] If we want to familiarize ourselves with that matrix on the basis of which *das Politische*, the sphere of the political, and the sphere of that homology, is formed, or with those fore-concepts with which we deal, if we want to understand where politics comes from, what its structures are, and how it is crystallized and manifested through the political, we must study Plato. […] So the first things we must get to know are Plato's writings.

2.

DECONSTRUCTION OF DEMOCRACY

The Concept of "Democracy" Is Not Neutral and Not Self-Evident

Democracy today cannot be discussed objectively. It is not a *neutral* concept: behind "democracy," as a political regime and corresponding value system, stands the West, Europe and the USA. For them "democracy" is a form of secular cult or a tool of political dogmatics, thus, to be fully accepted into society in the West, it is necessary by default to be "for" democracy. One who calls it into question falls out of the field of political correctness. Marginal opposition is tolerated; but if it is more than marginal, democracy sets its machines of oppression against its alternatives like any regime, any ideology, and any dominant religion. It is not possible to talk about "democracy" impartially. That is why in discussions about democracy we must say at once whether we are completely for or completely against it. I'll respond with extreme candor: I'm against it, but I'm against it only because the West is for it. I'm not prepared to accept anything thoughtlessly and uncritically on faith, even if everyone believes it, and all the more so if this is accompanied by a concealed (or clear) threat. You suggest that I rely on my own reason, no? I'll begin with the fact that reason advises me to reject all suggestions [*predlozheniy*, offers, proposals]. No one can give us freedom. It either is or it is not [we either have it or we don't]. A slave will convert even freedom into slavery, or at least into swinishness, and a free person will never be a slave even in fetters. From his time enslaved Plato did not become either less Plato or less free, while we still pronounce the name of the tyrant Dionysus with contempt, so which of them is a slave? At any rate, as a popular textbook on technical analysis says, "the majority is always wrong."

Only such critical distance in relation to "democracy" provides a field for its conceptual comprehension. We call "democracy" into doubt, into question, and challenge it as a dogma. We thus win the right to distance, but only in that way can we come to a valid and well-founded result. Not to believe in democracy does not mean to be its opponent. It means not to be its captive, not to be under its hypnosis and its suggestion. Starting from such unbelief and doubt, it is entirely possible that we'll conclude that democracy is something valuable or acceptable, or we might not. We should reason in exactly the same way about all other things. Only that is philosophy. There is no *a priori* evidence for a philosopher. It is exactly the same for a political philosopher.

It is worth recalling that democracy *is not a self-evident* concept. Democracy can be accepted or rejected, established or demolished. There were splendid societies without democracy and detestable ones with democracy, but there was also the opposite. Democracy is a human project, a construction, a plan, not fate. It can be rejected or accepted. That means it needs justification, apologia. If there won't be apologias for democracy it will lose its meaning. A non-democratic form of rule should not be taken as obviously the worst. The formula "the lesser evil" is a propagandistic ruse. Democracy is not the lesser evil … maybe it isn't evil at all, or maybe it is evil. Everything demands reconsideration.

Only from these two assumptions can we examine democracy carefully. It isn't a dogma, its imposition only repels one from it, and it has possible and entirely relevant and effective alternatives.

Elevating it into a dogma and denying its alternatives closes the very possibility of free philosophical discourse.

Demos in "Democracy": Aristotle's Etymology

Let us turn to the etymology of the word "demos," since "democracy" means "the rule of the demos." This word is most often translated by the word "*narod.*" However, in Greek there were many synonyms of the word narod: "ethnos," "laos," "phule," etc. "Demos" was one among them and had specific connotations. Initially "demos" described inhabitants, that is, people living in a concrete and entirely definite territory. As cities broadened, these territories began to be carved up inside the city, like today's regions or old-Russian city-parts [*gorodskiye kontsy*], so the inhabitants of one or another region were called a "demos."

In Julius Pokorny's *Indo-European Etymological Dictionary*, we see that the Greek "demos" stems from the Indo-European root dā (*də-) meaning "to divide," "to separate." With the formant "mo-" this makes the Greek "demos," and with the formant "lo-" the German *teilin* (divide) and Russian *delit'*.

Thus, in the very etymology of "demos" lies reference to something divided, cut into separate fragments and arranged on a certain territory. The closest in meaning is the Russian word population [*naselenie*] but by no means *narod*, since *narod* implies a cultural and linguistic unity, a community of historic being, and the presence of a certain destiny. A population (theoretically) can manage without that. "Population" refers to anyone who has settled or been settled on a given territory, but not one who is connected to that land by roots or the mark of citizenship [i.e. there are three distinct notions here: belonging by roots, belonging by the mere fact of settlement, and belonging through citizenship].

Aristotle, who introduced the concept of "democracy," regarded it extremely negatively, having in mind precisely this entirely Greek shade of meaning. According to Aristotle, "democracy" is practically identical with "mob rule," "ochlocracy (rule of the crowd)," since the population of a civic region consists of everyone without distinction. Aristotle opposes "democracy" as the worst form of rule not only compared with monarchy and aristocracy, corresponding to the rule of one or the best, which he regards, by contrast, positively, but also to "politeia" (from the Greek "polis," "city"). Like "democracy," "politeia" is the rule of many — not everyone without distinction, but the qualified ones, the rule of conscious citizens, differing from the rest by cultural and genealogical, as well as social and economic, indicators. Politeia is the self-rule of the citizens of the city, relying on traditions and foundations. Democracy is the chaotic agitation of a rebellious mob.

Politeia assumes the presence of cultural unity, a common historico-religious and cultic basis among citizens. Democracy can be established by an arbitrary collection of atomic individuals "distributed" into random sectors.

Aristotle, it is true, also knows other forms of unjust rule besides democracy: tyranny (rule of a usurper) and oligarchy (rule of a closed group of rich and corrupt scoundrels). All negative forms of rule are interconnected: tyrants often depend on precisely "democracy," just as "democracies" often appeal to oligarchy. Integrity, so important to Aristotle, is on the side of monarchy, aristocracy, and politeia. Division, fragmentation, partition into atoms, is on the side of tyranny, oligarchy, and democracy.

The Metaphysical Foundations of Democracy: The Hypotheses of the *Parmenides*

Let us turn to the metaphysical foundations of democracy. For this we will draw on the Platonic dialogue *Parmenides*. It is customary to distinguish two theses and eight hypotheses in it. The first thesis affirms the One. Four hypotheses follow (true, the Neo-Platonists added a fifth, but right now that's not crucial). The first thesis about the One and the four hypothesis following from it can be applied to the description of a republic [*gosudarstvo,* the word used to translate the dialogue by Plato called *Republic* in English; *gosudarstvo* can sometimes mean state in the narrow sense or, as in Plato, regime in the broad sense] based on hierarchy, stemming from the idea, the higher principle. The world built on affirmation of the One is built from top to bottom, from the One to the many. The same is true also of the republic, which reproduces the structure of the universe. At the head of such a republic are the monarch and priests, as servants of the One. Such a holy monarchy is simultaneously a model of the cosmos and a basis for the arrangement of the republic [*gosudarstvennogo ustroystva*]. The thesis about the One, and the hypotheses that follow from it, describe for us the spectrum of political models of traditional society, where the principle of integrity, the authority and sacral nature of power, and divine law predominated.

Sociologist Louis Dumont called such an approach based on the first thesis and four hypotheses "methodological holism," since the understanding of society is based on conviction in its organic, integral nature.

The second thesis in the *Parmenides,* and the second four hypotheses, stems from affirmation of the Many, other than the One. Here, at the basis of the perspective on the world, lies not unity, but plurality, atomism, and the play of fragments. Such a perspective leads to an atomistic perspective on the cosmos (the theory of Democritus) and to the justification of political regimes of precisely a "democratic" type, i.e. built not downwards from above, but upwards from below, not on the basis of the transition of the One into the many, but, on the contrary, in the opposite direction. Plato himself regarded the atomism of Leucippus and Democritus as a "heretical" teaching, and according to some sources, even encouraged the burning of their books in his Academy. In the Platonic understanding of the world, the society built on the principle of the Many (non-One) can similarly be regarded as a "political heresy."

Precisely this second thesis of the *Parmenides,* and the four hypotheses following from it, interest us now. Taking into account the first four, which relate to the monarchic cosmos, it is customary to call these the 5th, 6th, 7th, and 8th hypotheses of the *Parmenides*. If we consider them carefully, we will get four types of democracy, which are easy to discover in theory or practice in our surrounding world.

The Hypotheses of the *Parmenides* and Types of Democracy

The fifth hypothesis of the *Parmenides* is built on the assertion that although the One does not exist and the Many does, the One can be thought, realized, through relations within the Many. This can be interpreted simplistically as follows: although we begin with a plurality of atomic individuals, they can create something whole that would nevertheless be composite, collective, constructed. In political philosophy we see the classic example of socialism or social-democracy (in extreme form, communism) as a theory proposing to assemble out of separate individuals a solidary, "integral," but artificially integral, society, which in this case will be primary in relation to the individual and will educate this individual and form him. Both socialists and the first sociologists (Comte, in particular) thought of the political goal this way. The slogan of this approach can be the well-known motto: *Ex pluribus unum.*

Besides social democracy, the same principle applies to the political form of Hobbes's Republic [or State], his "Leviathan." Hobbes himself does not make anything more precise about the form of the political regime of the Republic [or State] because he was limited by the assertion that it is created through a social contract of persons striving to prevent the otherwise inevitable war of all against all. This principle — the One as a product of the agreement of the Many — thus also lies at the basis of modern theories of the Republic [or State]. It is clearest in social democracy. The conception of "*État-providence*," dear to the heart of the modern European, or the American "Welfare State," synthesizes both concepts (Republic [State] and sociality).

The sixth hypothesis says that the Many exists, and the One does not exist in itself or in its relations. This rejection of the construction of the One (artificial, collective, and mechanical) comprises the essence of another type of democracy, liberal democracy. It is characteristic of liberal democracy that it contests both the suggestion of the creation of a normative model of society insisted upon by socialists and social democrats, and (in the long term) the very existence of the Republic [or State]. We should not make from out of the Many One (*ex pluribus unum*); that is not at all necessary. The Many can fully remain Many, and the atomic individual can fully enjoy his complete freedom; thus, the Many rejecting the One gives us liberalism.

The seventh hypothesis of the *Parmenides* says: the Many exists, and through relations in it there is another Many. In other words, separate atoms, fragments, can ground the existence of other atoms, fragments, through relations among themselves. This gives us social and political models based on dialogue and communication. The One in this case is not constituted by a social contract, but instead a plurality of atoms constructs another plurality of atoms, which is

thereby endowed with being; thus arises the problem of the "Other,"
dialogue with [the other], and relations with [the other], who is today an extremely important center of a philosophical problem. "The
Other" [noun] and "the Other" [adjective] appear from the relations
of the Many. This model of "democracy" can be called "understanding
democracy" or "democracy of dialogue." It can full well be liberal, i.e.
in contrast to socialism, and not recognize society as a constructed
One. Instead of society, there can exist a communicational network,
structured in dependence on the spontaneous trajectories of free dialogues of separate individuals with one another in the field of "open
society." This is the model of "civil society." It is approximately how
representatives of the Chicago School of sociology imagine the state of
affairs (Mead in particular, with his symbolic interactionism).

Finally, the eighth hypothesis is the most "beastly." It says: the One
does not exist, but the Many does not create "another" Many and does
not construct it even in the process of relations inside the Many. Here
we get an extreme form of liberalism, repudiating altogether the figure
of the "Other." In political philosophy it corresponds to the "objectiv-
ism" of Ayn Rand and Alan Greenspan, the most extreme forms of
dehumanized individualism (characteristic of many Russian liberals).
De Sade's concept of the "sovereign individual," studied by Bataille and
Blanchot, belongs here. In this hypothesis there is only "the singular"
and its private property; everything else not only does not have being,
but is also not constructed artificially.

It is significant that Plato emphasized that these last four hypotheses are speculative and that the Many cannot exist without the One.
That is, the first thesis contains truth and the second falsehood, based
only on a game of the intellect.

The transition from traditional society to modern society, to modernity and to democratic, modernized republics [or states] is from
a philosophical perspective the transition from Plato's first thesis to

the second thesis, from the first four hypotheses to the second four. From every perspective — philosophical, sociological, culturological, etc. — modernity is based on the cult of "methodological individualism" and opposed to "methodological holism" (the first thesis and first four hypotheses). Precisely this rejection of the One, and acknowledgment of the primacy of the Many, is the basic dogma of the contemporary, the main postulate of modernity. In contemporary postmodernity precisely this approach is never contested. Postmodernity represents a hypertrophied, extravagant version of the last hypotheses of the *Parmenides*, the eighth in particular.

Political Platonism

The Platonic hypotheses help us understand the code of contemporary political philosophy. In the final analysis, all eight hypotheses can be regarded as fully rational models of the world and society and if we remove ourselves from the hypnotic suggestions of progress, we can fully make a conscious choice in favor of any of these hypotheses.

This means that we can select democracy, and any version of democracy, taking the position of the second thesis, or we can choose non-democracy, taking the position of the first thesis and acknowledge the One. What is interesting is that this choice can be made not only today, for it also stood before the people of Ancient Greece, who chose between Atlantis and Athens (the Platonic dialogue *Critias*), Athens and Sparta (the Peloponnesian War, praised by Thucydides), and the philosophy of the monarchists Plato and Aristotle and the liberal-atomists Democritus and Epicurus. While man remains man, he carries in himself, even if vaguely and distantly, a capacity for philosophy. That means that he carries in himself freedom of choice. Man can choose democracy, and one of its forms, or he can reject it.

At the same time, if we take the position of Plato and Platonism, then on the basis of the juxtaposition of democracy and the theses of the *Parmenides* we come to the conclusion that we live in a cosmos that cannot be: in a society built on an absolutely false dogma. Everyone today is regarded by default as a supporter of democracy. It would not be bad for those "by default" persons to become aware of the philosophical principles to which they are automatically (i.e. without being asked) ascribed.

On the other hand, all opponents of democracy are instantly enlisted in the class of persons professing an ideology the very name of which has long since become a curse-word and an insult, and unscrupulous hypnotists use this technique more and more. Instead of this word, grown hateful and made senseless, which I do not even wish to pronounce in this essay, it is better to call us "Platonists." Yes, we are bearers of *political Platonism*. We build our conception of the world and society starting from the first thesis of the *Parmenides* and the first four hypotheses. Others builds theirs starting from the second thesis and second four hypotheses. For heaven's sake — would it be so bad to know about this allegiance beforehand?

Being philosophers, that is free beings, we can full well say "yes" to the metaphysical status quo, consisting in the dogmatization of the second [thesis] of the *Parmenides* (i.e. democracy), but we can also say "no."

I say "no" to methodological individualism and the second thesis of the Platonic *Parmenides* and thereby clearly establish myself in the ranks, in the army of the supporters of Plato.

Plato burned the books of Democritus. Democrats, and in particular, Soros's spiritual guru Popper, in his catechism *The Open Society and its Enemies*, call to burn the books of Plato. Popper says directly: either enemies of the open society, liberal democracy, the second thesis of the *Parmenides*, or friends. This is a true war of hypotheses, a battle of epistemologies, a struggle of gnoseological paradigms, a fight of ideas.

Thus, for us, Platonists, *democracy is a false doctrine*; it is built on a world that doesn't exist and a society that cannot exist.

If that is so, the Platonist comes to a choice: democracy, by its false pretensions, conceals beneath itself something *else*, but something in any case very bad, unjust, and unhealthy, for instance a secret oligarchy or disguised tyranny, but that is a topic for another essay.

3.

POLITICAL PLATONISM AND ITS ONTOLOGICAL BASES

Part 1. Total Homologies of Power in Platonism

1. Platonism is based on the fundamental unity of the structures of knowledge, society, and cosmos. All these domains are three aspects of order.

2. The order of Platonism is based on a vertical topography, structured around the pairs: this — another, one — many, original (paradigm) — copy (*icon, eidolon*), idea — phenomenon.

3. A complete description of Plato's categories ([from] the dialogue *Parmenides*):

This (*tauta*) — another (*allo, eteron*);
One (*hen*) — many (*polla*);
Being (*on*) — non-being (*me on*);
Itself (*identitas, tauta*) — other (*alteritas, etera*);
Equal — unequal;
"Absolute" — "relative";
Resting — moving (*kinestai*);
Big (*megale*) — small;

Old/constant (*paleo*) — young/new (*neo*);

Indivisible/whole (*holon*) — divisible (partial);

Like (*homo*) — unlike (*me homo*);

Finite (*peiras*) — infinite (*apeiron*);

Intangible (*me aptesthai*) — tangible (*aptesthai*).

4. A vertical order extends between these categories. It descends from ideas to phenomena and ascends from phenomena to ideas.

5. This order predetermines the normative structure of man, world, society, and cognition. Man is a link in the chain of gods. He is stretched between origins [*nachala*], and he accomplishes by himself, by his existence, the transference of one into the other — like a demiurge, gods, luminaries [or celestial bodies: *svetila*]. He creates the order of the cosmos, organizes copies, and he dissolves phenomena in the contemplation of ideas. Creation (*poesis*) and contemplation (*noesis*) are man's two aspects.

6. The cosmos is a cosmos (i.e. beauty) because it is beautiful, and it is beautiful because it is ordered. It also has a structure from the meta-cosmos to the cosmos. At the center of the cosmos is the world soul, animating it. The cosmos is a big man [i.e. person, human, *chelovek*]. The cosmos is created by the demiurge (eternally) and is eternally dissolved in the luminous world of ideas.

7. Cognition is realized the same way: it brings ideas down to objects (theurgy, among Neo-Platonists) and raises objects to ideas.

8. The Republic [*Gosudarstvo*] — Politeia — is a slice of the cosmos (the Republic of souls, in the Platonist Chrysippus). Order is not reflected but *expressed* in it. The Republic (Platonopolis) is arranged from low to high and high to low (*poesis/noesis*). It establishes in law truths, given by philosophers; the impulse is delegated to guardians, and the artisans embody the directive

in the production of empirical things. Philosophers create the Republic demiurgically. The World Soul stands at the center of the Republic. This is the gold of being. It is the noetic concentration of the dynamic exchange between the world of ideas and the world of things. What is worthiest? The ideas. Who is occupied with them? Philosophers. The politeia is ordered when the worthiest is placed above and the least worthy below. Above are the ideas and those who contemplate them. Below are artisans, those who produce things.

9. Power in Platonism is sacral, rational, clear, and ideal. It is the crystallization of the world of paradigms. All the attributes of the One apply to power, hence it must be one [single], and monarchic. At the head of the philosophers stands the king of the philosophers, Prestor John, "the king of the world," *chakravarti*. The categories of the One apply to the king-philosopher.

10. Politics, as the art of the politeia, is the same as the art of philosophy. Not similar, but *identical*.

11. No will to power whatsoever. Power is truth. He who is in the domain of truth is already thereby in the domain of power. He who strives for power (truth) will never attain it. Truth (power) is like lightning. It is not, and then it is. And that is the event. It is not extended in time. It is vertical.

Part 2. The Structures of Platonopolis and the Hypotheses of the *Parmenides*

1. The homology of the politeia and ontology in Plato permits the application of the henology of the *Parmenides* to the structure of the Platonopolis (the normative case of the Politeia), leading us, thereby, to the Neo-Platonism of Plotinus and Proclus. Platonopolis should be constructed not only around the *Republic*,

Statesman, and *Laws*: [but on] Plato's teaching completely and coherently in all its aspects.

2. In that case in the bed of Platonopolis we can distinguish layers corresponding to the first four hypotheses of the *Parmenides*. Everything begins with the postulation of "*hen*," the One. Plato's Republic is a Republic of the One.

3. The first hypothesis postulates the transcendency of the One, which is "*epikeina ta panta*." That means that the normative Republic must be *open at the top*. It cannot be self-identical, since the One does not exist immediately. Hence, the Republic is built around something greater than itself. An apophatic hole must gape at the center of the Republic. Only then will the Republic be holy. That does not detract from the order of the political cosmos but on the contrary ensures its noetic respiration. Thus, the Republic should not be self-identical; it is always something *non-identical* to itself. This is not simply the Republic but the Republic of philosophers (the predicate is necessary). As soon as it becomes simply a Republic and self-identical, it at once loses the wave of ontological resonance with the paradigm and turns from a copy into a caricature, cartoon, parody, anti-politeia.

4. The second hypothesis. If the One is, it is Many. *Hen polla*. The Neo-Platonists interpreted this as the second hypostasis Nous. In the Republic, monarchy (*hen*) must be realized in the field of the philosophers as a noetic caste. There must be *many* philosophers around the throne of the king of philosophers. They make channels for him that are in contact with many things. But these channels must be intellective. The philosophers around the king of philosophers release [*snimayut*: also, remove, take off, gather] many things of the Republic by their awareness, harmonize them, open their eidetic sequences, and reveal their semantics.

5. The third hypothesis. One and Many. *Hen kai polla*. The Neo-Platonists interpreted this as the hypostatization of the World Soul, the third hypostasis of the Triad. *"Kai"* appears, the union "and." This is the union of guardians. With the philosophers, plurality exists in displaced form: intellectiveness (*noera*) displaces the particular (Many). Guardians encounter the Many as placed alongside. Their task is to marshal the Many. They guard the World Soul and do not allow the Many to overwhelm it. They destroy the superfluous. They transfer [*perevodyat*: transfer, translate] the Many into the One. The guardian stands between friends (Soul and philosophers) and enemies (the Many, detached phenomena pretending to be autonomous).

6. Iamblichus introduces between the third and fourth hypotheses an intermediate one. It can be related to the lower story of *hen kai polla* occupied by artisans. They also relate to the *"kai"* ("and"), but if guardians stand in the field of the *"kai"* closer to the *hen*, artisans (demiurges) are closer to the *polla*. They superimpose on the Many the *likeness* of the One, giving things and elements forms. Thereby they make things beautiful. Beauty is permeated by nostalgia. Nostalgia is the seal of the One. The artisans are artists, but they are lower than the guardians, because they are connected with matter. The first artists were blacksmiths. They descend into mines of matter (properly, *polla*, the fourth hypothesis) and procure metals therefrom. From metals they forge forms. Blacksmiths bear the seal of Tartarus. Hence guardians stand above them, and sometimes punish them.

7. The last level of Platonopolis is *polla*. That is plurality. This plurality is, because it is found inside the Republic, and the Republic is a form of existence of the One (*hen*). The many (*polla*) does not exist outside a correctly established Republic. In the Platonopolis,

to the many (*polla*) relate slaves, frogs, metals, animals, plants, soils, idlers, the ungifted, two-legged, three-legged, four-legged livestock, mosquitos, and civil society. All this, including moun- tains, lakes, seas, and clouds, has a *political significance*, since it relates to the field of the order-forming Polis. Without the Polis they lose ontology.

Part 3. The Aristomorphosis of Politics in Aristotle

1. Neo-Platonists *included* Aristotle in the context of Platonism; they did not exclude him. Porphyry's texts were ascribed in the Middle Ages to Aristotle. It was a platono-centric interpretation of Aristotelianism and the Stoics. Theoretically, there could also be another interpretation but now we will follow the Neo-Platonists.

2. Aristotle distinguishes three pejorative forms of rule: tyranny, oligarchy, and democracy, and three superior: monarchy, ar- istocracy, and politeia. I already spoke about the fact that the three pejorative forms relate to the second series of Parmenides's hypotheses — from the 5th to the 8th — based on rejection of the One. The politics of modernity strictly corresponds to these four hypotheses of a meontological character (as the Neo-Platonists thought). The analysis of the political deviancy of modernity led to the schema of the co-existence of all three pejorative types of the Political in the contemporary global model. At the center, the secret tyrant (the golden calf, the anti-Christ), around it the global oligarchy (multinational corporations, the hundred richest families in the world), and on the outer periphery, democracy as the power of the frenzied, swinish plebeians (who overthrew the feudal system of the guardians).

3. Professor Claudio Mutti, at a meeting of the Florian Geyer Club, justly noted that there is also an example of the superior, positive combination of these three regimes. He pointed to the Roman Empire. In it the principle of monarchy (the consul) was combined with aristocracy (senate) and the committees (politeia).

4. Developing Mutti's idea, we can correlate Platonopolis, based on the first four hypotheses of Parmenides, with the synthesis of the three superior forms of the Political in Aristotle. The monarchy of the king of philosophers can neighbor the assembly of guardians (the Gerousia of Sparta) and the local self-rule of artisans. We get a subsidiary imperial federalism in the spirit of Johannes Althusius.

5. Without monarchy, aristocracy will become oligarchy, politeia will degrade into democracy.

Conclusion

1. We obtained a structured system of political Platonism, complete and well-founded from every perspective.

2. It is entirely contrary to the spirit of modernity and post-modernity, which go against order, power, transcendency, sacrality, vertical topography, and models of homologies of man, world, politics, and knowledge.

3. The choice between political modernity and political post-modernity, which continues the anti-Platonic program of modernity, on one hand, and political Platonism, on the other, is a matter of free philosophical decision. Any effort to denounce political Platonism with reference to historical examples is nothing but empty and vacuous political propaganda, a primitive means to impose one's rightness by unfit methods of suggestion, pressure, and hypnosis, containing nothing rational, nothing philosophical, and nothing properly human. It is tendentiously interpreted

and deliberately selected facts torn from context, and accidental, unfounded generalizations of a purely rhetorical, not analytical character.

4. The construction of Platonopolis is an open, rational project. There are no arguments, none at all, for why not to be occupied with this, not to wish for it, not to believe in it, and not to strive for it. There is also nothing obligatory in this. This is precisely the domain of free political choice, carried out by a free being.

4.

TRADITIONALISM AGAINST DEVILOPOLIS

Reflections on the First Russian Congress of Traditionalists

From Progress to Eschatology: A Change of Reference Points

Today, more and more people are coming to the conclusion that humanity is not at all moving down the path it should be moving down, and that the promises of progress, development, and universal enlightenment have proved false or altogether unattainable. A hundred years ago a majority of people looked into the future with optimism, awaiting a transition to something better, in some sense guaranteed by the very logic of history. Today an entirely different mood prevails in societies: if it isn't directly apocalyptic, it is at least skeptical regarding the "unrestrained burst of humanity forward into progress and enlightenment." Although technical development continues at full speed, mechanisms are perfected, machines become "smarter," and means of communication improve their possibilities, this does not affect human happiness directly at all, does not guarantee any moral or spiritual heights, and does not increase justice in the social order. The Polish sociologist Piotr Sztompka correctly remarked that "if before the first quarter of the 20th century the idea of progress prevailed in the humanities, later the theory of cyclical crises and the theory of catastrophes became more popular."

If at the beginning of the century only a few intellectuals struggled with anxiety about the problematic future of humanity, like Spengler, who pronounced the "Decline of the West," or Nietzsche, who pointed to the rise of nihilism and "the death of God," then in our days the sense of catastrophe is becoming widespread in the broadest spheres. It is penetrating into mass culture and becoming the prevailing out-look. The promised eternal world, humanism, justice, the constant growth of wealth, the eradication of poverty, the impending moral ascent of humanity — these are no longer expected to ever be realized. Alienation grows alongside the improvement of technical devices, technology displaces life, and new scientific achievements are used for the perfection of the military complex of global, hegemonic states. The more the talk of peace and calm, the greater the bloody sacrifices and violence.

Now is the time to start thinking about how to explain such a turn. What are its ideational bases? After all, the obvious psychologi-cal condition should be accompanied by more systematic, structural principles that raise all of that into a system. Just as hopes for the bright future gave rise to the theory of progress, so shouldn't the growth of skepticism and disappointment lead us to a theory of regress?

Traditionalism as Philosophy and Its Appearance in Russia

Such a theory, in fact, has long since been created and developed, although it was until very recently the property of a relatively narrow circle of intellectuals. I'm talking about traditionalism: a philosophy, worldview, ideology, style. It's time to give it more steadfast attention.

Although traditionalism came to Russia more than twenty years ago, when the first translations of the classics of this philosophy were made (the texts of René Guénon, Julius Evola, Mircea Eliade, Titus Burckhardt, etc.), the first texts of properly Russian traditionalists, and the first representative conference of traditionalists, occurred altogether recently, in the fall (October 2011). Several eminent figures of the European branch of this movement — notably, a sheikh of the Sufi order 'Abd al-Wājid, Sergio Yahya Pallavicini, Claudio Mutti, traditionalist publisher and professor, and publisher and scholar Christian Boucher — as well as Russian traditionalist philosophers participated. Although in the congress almost a hundred papers and presentations on the classical themes of this movement were discussed — Tradition against the modern world, society's loss of the spiritual, the vertical, and the notion of sacral order, critiques of Western civilization, and studies in the domain of traditional religions (Orthodoxy, Islam, Judaism, etc.) — some unconventional themes were also raised: the metaphysical interpretation of postmodernity, the philosophy of chaos, and the structural-linguistic analysis of religion and spiritual philosophies. The organizers of the conference also accented the philosophy of Plato and its influence on classical religions and various philosophical systems.

Twenty years is a relatively short period of time for a difficult-to-understand doctrine to be introduced, and then disseminated by conferences for Russian assimilation. Nevertheless, as the European classics of this approach noted, the Russian school of traditionalism has not only been successful, but represents an original, living, and to a significant extent, reactive orientation, absorbing into its ranks many intellectual youths, students, graduate students, and scholars. The connection of Russian traditionalism with the academic milieu, not usual for Western representatives of this movement, were underscored by the fact that the organizers of the conference were the sociological faculty of Moscow State University together with the Center for Conservative Research, which has been very actively engaged with traditionalism in recent years. Many doctors and candidates of sciences, graduates, and students participated in the work of the conference. Academic interest in traditionalism was vividly demonstrated.

The well-known traditionalist and conference participant Claudio Mutti spoke as follows in the final plenary session about the state of contemporary Russian traditionalism:

> I'm amazed by what I've seen here, coming to Moscow twenty years after my first visit. Twenty years ago this country was falling apart, and strange people were walking the streets. I couldn't imagine that twenty years later questions of traditionalism would be interpreted here on such a level and with such enthusiasm. This differs significantly from all traditionalist events I've attended in Western Europe. I'd like to note that when we talk about the discussion of those questions of traditionalism that were raised in this conference, an altogether different atmosphere prevails in Western Europe. First, the audience there, even in large European capitals, has practically no chance of gathering as many people interested in the problematic of traditionalism as here, but most of all I'm impressed by the elaborateness and depth with which the participants expounded their arguments. Second, while in Western Europe traditionalism is mainly a conservative movement, which insists either on the preservation of what is or the reproduction of what was, or is a sort of alibi for many to do nothing, here, in Russia, I saw that traditionalism is permeated by a creative, innovative spirit. Even the very fact that this conference is dedicated to postmodernity is a sign of the creativity and originality of the approach.

René Guénon: The Foundations of Philosophy

So, what is traditionalism? It is a school [of thought] associated with the works and ideas of the French philosopher René Guénon (1886–1951). If we look at Guénon from a sociological point of view, he will not seem to be quite the complex and confused mystic he is sometimes made to be. Moreover, while being an extreme conservative, Guénon in many respects anticipated the philosophical methodology of postmodernity, though in a very peculiar sense.

The essence of Guénon's theories consisted in the following. There are two types of society, traditional and modern, entirely different in their basic arrangements, value systems, and socio-political modes (any humanities scholar or sociologist would agree), but the majority of people today automatically identify with modern society and un-critically absorb, through suggestion, the arrangements of the modern world. Thus modern man also forms an impression about the world of Tradition, about traditional society, starting from a completely pre-given basis: traditional society is seen by default as something under-developed, dark, based on superstition and irrational assumptions, as something unscientific, uncivilized, and technologically backward. In other words, traditional society is thought of as the first step of a pro-gram, preceding "real society," the society of modernity. This approach is based on axiomatic acceptance of the claim that the world develops in the direction of perfection (from small to large, from worse to bet-ter, from simple to complex) and that progress governs the course of world history.

René Guénon proposed looking at things from an opposite per-spective. He showed that progress is nothing but an ideology, a social model for explaining complex processes around us, and so it cannot be taken as an axiom. It is a hypothesis, nothing more, which won for itself the right to be a dogma during the course of what Guénon thought was not an altogether fair fight, hence the lack of understand-ing about Tradition and its values, the idolatry of material, time, technique, individualism, and the series of ever newer automatons. We need only discard the prejudices of progress, however, and the world will reveal itself in a new light. Traditional society will prove to be not "insufficiently modern" but simply radically other, based on eternity, sacrality, hierarchy, appeal to God and the spirit, and not to matter and sense experience. We need only tear our gaze away from the earth towards the sky to understand that precisely Tradition, including religious tradition, says what our soul requires from itself, about spirit, about being, about the world, and about God, while modern society serves only corporeal needs. At the same time, the value of the body and lower psychic impressions are not only taken into account but begin to prevail and displace spiritual values. With modernization comes a total break with the world of being, the Primordial. Man is distanced from his archetype. Society loses order and is scattered into fragments, atoms, parts, and individuals. Tradition is integrity [wholeness]. Modernity is entropy, dispersion, and dissipation elevated into the rank of a value and actively spread everywhere.

Thus, in his work *Crisis of the Modern World* Guénon provides a devastating critique of the basis of all of Western civilization, predicting its impending and inevitable end. At the same time, he advances an alternative system of values found in traditional society, established on the foundations of religion, spirit, faith in hierarchy, and metaphysics. In this way, the proportions are reversed: instead of the idea of progress, customary for modern people, and the placement of modern society above traditional society, Guénon advances the directly opposite idea that modernity is not progress but regress, decline, the fall of humanity into the abyss of matter, sensuality, corporeality, and mechanicalness. Modernity is the degradation of Tradition; progress is the collapse of values, and a path into the abyss. Accordingly, those forces, philosophies, and socio-political tendencies that are oriented toward the modernization of traditional society are, according to Guénon, bearers of evil perversion leading humanity to its death. For Guénon everything modern is depraved, everything traditional deserves respect and veneration. Religion, hierarchy, sacrality, and metaphysics are true;

democracy, profanism, and rationalism are false. We get a radically new perspective on the essence of the historical process: it is not a path upwards, but a slide down, not a drawing near to the truth, but a falling away from it, not a movement to spiritual horizons, but immersion into the material abysses of nothing.

Can this last long, Guénon asks? And he answers: no, it can't. We stand face to face with a fateful feature of Western civilization that carries the rest of the world with it. In his fundamental book, *The Reign of Quantity and the Signs of the Times,* Guénon depicts the material world as a "great parody" that must come to the final limit of materialism and atheism. In this parody we recognize the figures of traditional religious eschatology, the figure of the anti-Christ, for Christians, the Dajjal, for Muslims, and the "erev rav," the great confusion of the Kabbalists.

What should we do? Guénon suggests that it is too late to do anything; nothing can stop the West in its expansions, in its globalization. It is a matter for unique personalities capable of recognizing the entire drama of the historical situation to exert heroic efforts to tear themselves from the captivity of modernity's hypnosis, to unite into a sacral elite of the end times, and to raise the flag of traditionalism as the final custodian of the holy before the face of hell arises. The community of traditionalists, those professing traditional religions and able to recognize the true character of the surrounding world, becomes, in his theory, the "ark of salvation."

In the end, though, Guénon's philosophy is optimistic. After describing the horrors of the modern world and its inevitable collapse, he declares that all cosmic manifestations are nothing but illusions, and beyond the end of this world another begins. The truth always remains eternal and hidden behind the veil of a mirror game, but the spirit of metaphysics is capable of penetrating into it even in the most difficult circumstances.

Guénon himself converted to Islam, moved to Cairo, became a Sufi sheikh, and broke for good with the West and with Western society, which he regarded as the source of the global infection of the spirit. By his example he showed how it is possible to leave the modern world of the West and find a spiritual homeland in the East which is, as of now, less permeated by the devilish structures of modernity.

Julius Evola's *Revolt Against the Modern World*

Guénon's followers drew various conclusions from his worldview. Some followed their teacher into Islam. Others tried to apply his ideas to Christianity and Judaism. Significant, too, is the case of his follower, the Italian traditionalist Julius Evola (1898–1974), who can rightfully be regarded as the second most eminent figure after Guénon in this school. By temperament a warrior and soldier, Evola did not agree with the passive rejection of modernity but proposed to put up a fight, to join with the European Conservative Revolution movement in order to challenge it, and to try to revive society on principles of Tradition, despite the difficult circumstances of modernity. Evola asserted that the West was first to descend into the phase of perversion, decline, and degradation, having adopted the decadent values of democracy, liberalism, humanism, and materialism, but that it is also destined to be the first to exit the crisis. Evola called not only for the recognition of the "crisis of the modern world," but for revolt against it, too. Thus, his major work is called *Revolt Against the Modern World*. In it he describes the structure of traditional society, shows the trajectory of its degeneracy and collapse, and outlines a plan for the restoration of Tradition in the course of an active and full-blooded metaphysical and spiritual, but also political and existential struggle. Evola was convinced that it was necessary to destroy the root of European decline and return to Europe's spiritual foundations, reestablishing a sort of "New Middle Ages."

Evola tried to embody his ideas by the most diverse means and despite the failure of some political efforts connected one way or another with the Conservative Revolution in the 20th century, he remained true to his initial plans of giving traditionalism a practical, operational dimension, of changing both the outside world and the subject himself. At the end of his life Evola concentrated on the strategy of "riding the Tiger" (as one of his later works is called), which is to say not simply to oppose the tendencies of modernity, but to stand on the side of certain revolutionary tendencies directed against the modern world, though not for conservative reasons, and later to shift them into another direction. Thus, he advanced the thesis of the "differentiated man," who is able to preserve a vertical posture among the collapsing, disintegrating world of modern liberal degradation. Arthur Moeller van den Bruck, another conservative revolutionary, also advanced the idea that: "Formerly, conservatives strove to oppose revolutions, but we must join them, and be at the head of them, and lead them into a different direction." Evola's late ideas fit this logic perfectly.

Traditionalism and Non-Conformism

Guénon and Evola had a tremendous influence on certain circles of Western intellectuals. They inspired many philosophers, in particular, René Daumal, Georges Bataille, and Gilbert Durand; André Gide, Antonin Artaud, Ezra Pound, Jean Parvulesco, and Éric Rohmer were under their influence. Of course, on account of their radical critique of modernity and its foundations, they could not count on broad dissemination or a deserving place in the general context of modern philosophy. All those who were interested in non-conformism, however, those who strove to get out from under the oppressive frames of liberal political correctness, could not pass them by indifferently. They either filled such people with hatred, or, on the contrary, seized them.

Regardless, in the course of a century, the philosophy of traditionalism took shape as a kind of independent ideational movement [i.e. school of thought]. It was discovered in Russia by members of the so-called Yuzhinsky Circle (Mamleev, Golovin, Dzhemal) in the 1960s, but the works of traditionalists started to be published at the end of the 1980s.

Reasons for the Relevance of Traditionalism

In our time all the conditions are present to give this philosophy heightened attention. This is important to do for the following reasons:

1. The crisis of modern civilization, the inner contradiction of Western ideology, clearly obvious dual standards of international politics, and the moral crisis of technological society are evident. These things are no longer possible to deny. In order to correctly comprehend and describe what we are dealing with, to accurately comprehend the crisis of the modern world, theoretical philosophical instruments are necessary to help us find the right formulas. Formerly this function was served in part by Marxist criticism, which strictly criticized liberal capitalism, concealing even more painful contradictions, but in our time the ideational potential of Marxism as a critical theory has been exhausted. It lacks the correct means to describe the processes unfolding in the modern world, and it received a very difficult, or even fatal, blow in the collapse of the socialist system. As a result, critique from the left is becoming unpopular. The time of critique from the right is arriving. The French traditionalist René Alleau foresaw this when he wrote his highly astute article "Guénon and Marx," which showed the similarity of these thinkers in their relentless critique of the Western bourgeois world. Indeed, this criticism is even more total in Guénon.

2. Alongside disappointment in progress, the influence of conservative ideas is increasing, but conservatism will remain vapid if it insists on only the presently existing state of affairs, the status quo. What exists now will change, which means that the conservative ideology will also change, so it is necessary to turn toward deeper values, unchanging and related to eternity. That is precisely what traditionalism proposes to do in its fundamental critique of historical time, rejection of progress, and apologia for the invariable vertical spiritual order. With traditionalism's uncompromising faith in, and summons to a return to, the roots, customs, and religion and its invariable truths, traditionalism is the core of consistent conservatism.

3. Russia must choose its path in a rapidly deteriorating world. This deterioration presents itself as technical and social improvement, but in fact it leads the situation to an ever greater dead-end. The creation of a speculative financial economy drove the global economy into a deep crisis. The American model of controlling the world through the control of finances and the reserve currency brought many countries, including the US itself, to the brink of bankruptcy. In this situation, what is necessary are not technical measures, but some kind of radical decision, a certain decisive turnabout. Traditionalism offers the entire necessary philosophical, ideational, conceptual, and sociological apparatus for that.

That is the relevance of traditionalism, and that is why the first congress of traditionalists in Russia took place at the right time, precisely when the right historical circumstances were there.

Towards Political Platonism

In the world of ideas and philosophical concepts, time flows differently than it does in ordinary life. A minor change in the structure of one or another theory, or an original formation of concepts or philosophical speculations, can bring about very serious changes, so it would be too naïve to await ready-made decisions from the traditionalist congress; but nevertheless, there were such results.

First, many presenters set themselves the task of showing that the philosophical background of Guénon and his followers' traditionalism is extremely close *to the Platonic tradition* and its full-fledged, and radical, idealism, as well as its assertion of the invariability of the world of principles, ideas, models, and the circulation of reflections in the world of phenomena and material bodies. The further a copy moves from the original, the more it loses its similarity to it and the more isolated it becomes from it. Thereby it loses its meaning, essence, being, beauty, and verity.

In other words, traditionalism can be taken as radical Platonism, and, consequently, it can qualitatively enrich its language through broad appeal to Platonic sources in the most diverse traditions, from the Christian dogmatics of the Cappadocian Fathers to the mysticism of Dionysius the Areopagite or to the Hesychasts. In Islam, besides the philosophers proper, al-Farabi or Ibn Sina, Platonism permeates the Sufi tradition, Shiite gnosis, and the philosophy of Ishraq. In Judaism, Platonism is the basic map for the Kabbala and its theories of emanation. Thus, Platonism provides a serious philosophical basis for the development of dialogue of traditional confessions to the extent that they strive to defend their identity and withstand the pressure of secular globalization. On a dogmatic basis, inter-confessional dialogue beyond a certain point is not possible because of the fear of losing identity and falling into syncretism. A properly traditionalistic language is too extravagant and sophisticated to be applied universally, but read through the eyes of traditionalists who have first digested Guénon and Evola, precisely Platonic philosophy provides the basis for the elaboration of a consolidated position of all those forces in the world that stand on the side of the sacral.

Moreover, armed with Platonism, traditionalism can easily enter the academic sphere and present its perspectives in a language considered appropriate in that domain.

This conclusion will still need to be defended and secured, but the direction has been set. In the most extreme and radical case we can speak of political Platonism and even of Platonic revolution.

Critique of Devilopolis: Opening the "World Egg" from Below

Another highly significant conclusion from the traditionalist congress concerned the understanding of the phenomenon of postmodernity. Guénon describes the historical process as three states of the "Cosmic Egg," a figure adopted from the Orphic and Hindu traditions; there are echoes of this symbolism in the tradition of painting eggs during Easter. In the normal case (traditional society), the "World Egg" is open from the top, and rays of the primordial (God) penetrate into the world directly, making each thing a symbol, a reflection, a manifestation of higher being. That is the sacral world, the Universe [*Vselennaya*] awash in the sacred light. The second condition corresponds to the modern world: the "World Egg" is closed at top. Rays no longer reach things. Each thing begins to signify only itself. That is the profane (non-sacral) order, the epoch of materialism, rationalism, and humanism, but in his book, *The Reign of Quantity and the Signs of the Times,* Guénon describes another condition, which he locates in the future (he died in 1951). That is the opening of the "World Egg" from below, when things begin to serve as support not for divine [*nebesnykh*] influences, but for the direct invasion of democratic essences. Things become not only

non-sacral (profane), but "possessed," "demoniac." Guénon calls this
last phase of history "the great parody." In Christianity, it is described
as the epoch of the Antichrist. The Antichrist parodies Christ.

This corresponds to the traditionalist interpretation of postmodernity. Instead of the ideal traditionalistic caste republic [*gosudarstvo*,
state], described also by Plato, instead of Platonopolis we are wit-
nesses of the appearance of the anti-republic, and the anti-polis, the
Devilopolis. This is a type of socio-political system in which all threads
lead not to the unified source [*edinoe nachalo*] ("symbol," in Greek,
means "uniting") but to division, corruption, decomposition, entropy,
and dispersion (and in Greek this is "devil," from "diabol-," i.e. "dividing," "disuniting.")

Thus, traditionalists should reconsider somewhat the classical critique of modernity, which the founders of this philosophy formulated,
and move towards a critique of postmodernity, which means that not
profanism, but parody, simulacrum, and counterfeit become the main
enemies of traditionalism and the main features of Devilopolis.

Not the profane, but the pseudo-sacral, not atheism, but pseudo-
religion, not the strict dictates of materialistic dogmas, but the soft
"permissiveness" of an indifferent open society — this is what represents the main challenge for traditionalism.

The Devil is described in Tradition as a mocker and as an ape of
God. Today's cult of humorists, whose jokes are gradually becoming
less funny, more stupid and base, and from that more ominous, is
highly significant in this regard.

One presentation suggested the idea that in the structure of
Devilopolis things acquire a common quantitative equivalent, a
price. The reduction of things to money, and money to collections
of numbers or to a barcode, is the expression of their integration in
Devilopolis, a mechanism of their penetration by a ray from "beyond,"
breaking forth from under the bottom of the "World Egg." A thing

loses its real value the moment when it acquires a price and, accordingly, a price tag, but our civilization is built wholly and completely on money. It is the civilization of Mammon. It is not possible to serve God and Mammon simultaneously.

Thus, the traditionalist and conservative approach leads us to the field of social criticism, the calcification of capitalism, and opposition to the modern economic system.

Russia's Eschatological Choice

Surprisingly, little was said at the conference about Russia (compared to similar events where Russian intellectuals gather). This is significant. Russia is a part of the modern and post-modern world. Whether we like it or not, the processes occurring in the West exert a strong influence on us. Whether we strive to imitate the West openly (modernization, liberalization, Westernization) or think about adapting Western technologies to national interests, we are captive to Western concepts, Western sciences, Western theories, and Western language. Since that is so, we are on the periphery of Devilopolis, not an alternative to it, but one of its remote provinces preserving, by inertia, some ties with traditional society, not through our own will, resolve, or choice, but because the tendencies and directives from the "center" reach us with difficulty and haphazardly. Russia is not the anti-West, but the not-quite-West [*nedo-Zapad*, *nedo*, under, as in under-developed, on its way towards, but falling short of]. Elites would like to see it as "the West," but they understand it very poorly, while the masses, it seems, don't understand anything at all.

Postmodernity comes to us through mass media, styles, habits, modes, computer networks, and youth culture but at the same time it is far from being understood or sounded out. What is more, society on the whole is in a state of indecision: it no longer strives "beyond the border," as it did in the 90s, nor does it yearn to imitate the West in everything, but it also cannot consolidate itself around some sort of alternative, cannot insist on its unique identity [*samobytnost'*, self-being; originality, identity], since this unique Russian identity is elusive and distinct.

Yes, we have not proceeded as far along the path of collapse as Western society has done, but that does not mean that we are full of resolve to avoid that path, or to consciously choose Tradition. Of course not, and that is wrong.

If Russia wants to survive spiritually, it must stand under a different banner, under the banner of Tradition, radical conservatism, Orthodox faith in union with other traditional confessions, and, if you like, under the banner of "Revolution against the post-modern world." Those who have discovered for themselves the traditionalist worldview have made such a choice.

Ahead are a crisis and the quick end of the known order. Guénon asserted with full justification that this wretchedness cannot last long. All the signs of the times are present. The people of Platonopolis have made their choice. The powers of Devilopolis have chosen a different fate for all the others.

Does Russia have a chance to turn to another path? This chance always exists where there is will, intellect, and resolve. We need only transform our apparent deficiency (lag) into our merit and take the decisive step, not forward (the abyss is there), but… into eternity (you thought backwards, but not backwards).

5.

PLATO'S RELEVANCE FOR RUSSIA AND THE PLATONIC MINIMUM

1. Plato's teaching is an account of the Universal [*Vselennoy*] Logos, thorough and exhaustive. All philosophy is constructed in relation to Plato. It is always either a continuation of him, a contestation of him, or both. This is evident already in Aristotle, where he does exactly this: he both continues and contests him. He is the first post-Platonist. Knowledge of Plato is the fundamental basis for all knowledge of the humanities [*gumanitarnogo znaniya*; *gumanitarnoe* can mean, liberal in the sense of liberal education, thus classical, also humanitarian, humanistic]. If we fail to pay due attention to Plato, we will never be full-fledged participants in the scientific Universe. Anyone who does not know or understand Plato cannot know or understand anything. Plato is the creator of the fundamental field [*bazovoy topiki*] of philosophy. Philosophy, in its turn, is the field [*topika*] of theology, science, and politics. Plato, then, lies at the basis of theology, science, and politics. Lying at the basis, however, does not mean that Plato exhausts philosophy. He is not the end, but rather the beginning.

All initial contact with science, religion, politics, philosophy, or sociology begins with precisely Plato. This fact, however, has become effaced. Among us, Plato is forgotten and not understood. With him forgotten, we do not exist [*nas ne sushchestvuyet*].

2.	Today we often meet scholars, politicians, sociologists, religious figures, or intellectuals who are not familiar with Plato or do not understand him. Such people should be promptly removed from the state. Even traffic police must know Plato.

3.	The most important works of Plato are the *Timaeus* and *Republic*. Here the very field [*topika*] of his philosophy is set forth, the framework in which everything else unfolds. Of secondary concern is the question: is Plato the creator of this field? This is not ultimately important: it is known in connection with his name. Judging by the chain Plato-Plotinus-Gemistus Pletho, "Plato" could full well be a "status," "office," or even "function" (similar to what Guénon has said about Zoroaster and the many "Zoroasters").

4.	The work [*topika*] *Timaeus* depicts a hierarchy of three principles [*nachal*]. This is a vertically differentiated symmetrical world with three ontological layers. All three layers are eternal and exist always. Where one exists, the other two also exist. Plato is trichotomous. The three principles are ideas-phenomena-space (*Khôra*).

5.	Ideas are blinding, flying sparks of the eternal and immutable light. They are the most important. They are the ones that are, that exist. They are models, paradigms, and rays. They comprise the Logos. Ideas are grasped by the higher intellect or intellectual intuition. When a person encounters the ideas, they paralyze him. It is like erotic feeling in its culmination, but intensified a hundredfold. Encounter with the ideas changes a person irreversibly. The idea is the highest value. It serves nothing, and it belongs to no one. It has no practical significance. On the contrary, everything that exists serves the ideas. The idea is Master [*Gospodin*].

6. Phenomena (appearances) are mere copies of the idea. They are slaves of the idea. They are corrupt ideas, vague ideas, and they are clothed in burdensome dust. They are perceived by the senses. Phenomena do not have their own being. Their individuality is a defect in relation to their idea. A good slave serves well, a bad one badly. In a good slave, the will of the Master is apparent, but in a bad slave, only his own laziness is apparent. Bad phenomena are individualistic, while Good ones are functional. Rain is either Divine Rain, and good, or a source of obtrusive wetness. Phenomena are set out in eidetic ranks. The threads connecting copies with ideas unite things into these ranks. Some phenomena ascend the eidetic chain to one idea, while other groups of phenomena ascend to another.

7. On the border between copies and ideas stands the Platonic "goddemiurge." He injects ideas into phenomena; he is on the side of the ideas. On the side of the phenomena, the philosopher-person, a phenomenal God, fulfills the symmetrically reverse function. He elevates phenomena through the eidetic ranks to the ideas. He injects things into the sphere of the origin. He consumes and devours [*zhret*]. The philosopher is a king-sacrificer [*tsar'-zhrets*; *zhrets*: priest, sacrificer]. He returns things to the zone of primordial fire. Plato's republic is divine, philosophical, fiery, and eschatological. The republic is fire. It must consume things so that from them ideas are born, as their masters.

8. There is also *Khôra*. *Khôra* is a receptacle, a mother, and a wet nurse. It is matter. *Khôra* is the place where phenomena (appearances) are disclosed. The *Timaeus* argues that for there to be an

appearance, there must be a place where the appearance appears. *Khôra* is the most difficult [principle]. It is grasped not by intellectual intuition like the ideas and not by the senses (perception) like phenomena, but by a "bastard Logos," (*logos nothos*). It is connected with the element of sleep [or dream]. ("We are such stuff as dreams are made on," says Prospero in Shakespeare's *Tempest*). *Khôra* is chaos seen from without, from the perspective of Logos. In Plato's topography [*topika*], *Khôra* has no depths; it is the lowest layer of the world of copies, phenomena.

9. Plato's topics [*topika*] are learned through initiation. This is initiatory knowledge. At its basis lies the experience of the idea [and] the capacity for a trichotomous division of appearances into idea, appearance itself, and *Khôra*. An appearance breaks down into the components: what appears and to whom, but the idea is not a subject or a property of a subject. The idea is that which constitutes subject and object. Both subject and object are appearances, i.e. copies. The idea is radically transcendent. Contact with it is the remelting of the phenomenon in the fire of the intellect. Science is based on the dramatic and traumatic experience of initiation.

10. A few conclusions about the relevance of Plato follow from the preceding:

    ▪ Without a thorough comprehension of Plato, science is not actual even in relation to the so-called natural sciences; accordingly, in our country, where there is a problem with the Logos, it is necessary to introduce a *Platonic minimum*, without which the professional occupation of science and full participation in the Higher School should be made unacceptable. One can reject, critique, refute, develop, or overthrow Plato, but he must first be understood.

- Without a correct understanding of Plato, politics is not satisfactory. All politicians should likewise pass a *Platonic minimum*; since the Republic is an idea and politicians are part of the Republic, they must be familiar with the experience of the idea, otherwise they should get out of politics and sell mobile phones.

- Without knowledge of Plato's foundations, religion is intellectually powerless. Even Orthodox theology is based on the Platonic teaching [*topika*]. Without knowledge of Plato, Christianity remains approximate. For ordinary Christians, this is not obligatory and they can absorb elements of Platonism through sacred tradition, i.e. mediately and fragmentarily, but for the clergy it is obligatory.

- The philosophy of chaos is bound to the Platonic field [*topika*] in an opposite way: it is built within *Khôra* as a volumetric principle, overturning the Platonic field [*topika*] and considering it *de profundis*. Heidegger proposes to create a "philosophy of another beginning" on an anti-Platonic revolution; to effect such a revolution, it is necessary to know and understand Plato.

11. Without Plato, Russian society can [*sc*: last, continue, exist] no more. Everything will be mixed: conservatism, modernization, technology, science, economics, politics, innovation, social problems, efforts to create something worthwhile of its own or to accurately copy something foreign.

12. The project of a New Russia must begin with the *Platonic announcement*.

6.

CHRISTIANITY AND NEO-PLATONISM

Theses by Alexander Dugin

1. Neo-Platonism is the intellectual milieu in which the formation of Christian theology took place. It is incorrect to reduce Neo-Platonism only to Origen or Dionysus the Areopagite and to the Christian mystics. It is much broader than that. Neo-Platonism, understood in a Christian way, is precisely the foundation of the conceptual apparatus of the entire Nicene dogmatics [*dogmatika*; there is a usual Russian term for the Nicene Creed, and this isn't it], so familiarity with Neo-Platonism as a philosophy, and also as a way of thought and even way of life, is absolutely necessary for the Christian.

2. Neo-Platonism relates to Orthodoxy in various ways, and we can understand it to mean different things, both broadly and narrowly:

    ▪ In the broadest sense: as the thought of the Hellenes, and Hellenism as such, i.e. the milieu (social, intellectual, cultural, philosophical, aesthetic) in which Christianity was established;

- as the Alexandrian school of thought from Philo of Alexandria to Clement and Origen (like Plotinus, Origen was a student of Ammonius Saccas);

- as the allegorical and symbolic interpretation of the Bible (in opposition to the exegetical practices of the School of Antioch);

- as Philo of Alexandria's Hellenistic interpretation of the Bible (as a Jewish precedent for later Christian exegesis);

- as Origen and the origin of Origenism;

- as the framework of the Cappadocian Fathers (Saint Basil the Great, Saint Gregory of Nyssa, and Saint Gregory of Nazianzus);

- as the influence of Plotinus, Porphyry, Amelius, etc. on Christian authors (those same Cappadocian Fathers);

- as Dionysus the Areopagite and Proclus's influence on him;

- as John Philoponus and his polemic with Proclus from Christian positions;

- as Saint Maximus the Confessor;

- as Michael Psellos and John Italus;

- as Hesychasm and the theory of uncreated light;

- and as Gemistus Pletho and the Mystras School.

3. These concern Orthodoxy in its Greek derivation. There was also Neo-Platonism in the West, and it is not possible to make a sharp distinction before the Great Schism, so we should include also the Western fathers, Saint Augustine, Boethius, Scotus Erigena.

4. Platonism also influenced scholasticism after the great schism (but in a different, Post-Schism, Catholic context) and served as a specific worldview in the Renaissance (Ficino, Pico della Mirandola).

5. In the era of the emergence of Russian religious philosophy (in the 19th and 20th centuries), all these lines one way or another influenced sophiology and everything connected with it. That means, first, that Russian philosophy is inextricably connected with Neo-Platonism and, second, that so too is the entire culture of the Silver Age.

6. It is appropriate to ask: where is the place of Neo-Platonism in all its senses in contemporary Christian self-consciousness? In the West, Catholic thought, even in its most conservative form, as a rule, stops with Thomism and scholasticism, while the mystical tendencies of a more radical Platonism are examined in a different, either scientific or spiritualistic, context. In the East and in Orthodoxy on the other hand, one gets the impression that the theme of Neo-Platonism is not systematically emphasized at all.

7. For contemporary Russian Orthodoxy, a new familiarity with Neo-Platonism and its topics [*topiki*] is vitally important. We can draw up a plan for its step-by-step realization:

- Platonic studies (including study of the Greek language and original Platonic terminology);

- the study of the Neo-Platonic heritage (Plotinus, Iamblichus, Proclus);

- the delineation of Neo-Platonic tendencies in the most important lines of Orthodox thought and dogma;

- the reconsideration of Russian religious philosophy (Solovyov, Bulgakov, Florensky, Losev) from the perspective of a broad knowledge of Platonism;

- the creation of a school of Orthodox Neo-Platonism.

8. An extremely important element is the task of the precise reconstruction of the condemnation of Platonism and Origenism at the

time of Justinian, the condemnation of John Italus, the Hesychast
controversy, and the battle against Imiaslavie [onomatodoxy]. It
is necessary to reconstruct precisely the context, meaning, and
aims of all these moments, in order to execute a deconstruction.
We must understand the structure and ideational bases of the
criticism of Platonism at various stages of the establishment of
Christian dogma and Christian history as such.

9. It is useful to carry out a comparative analysis of how Neo-
    Platonist tendencies played out in other monotheistic religions:
    in Islam (al-falasifa, at-tasavvuf, Ishrak, Shiite gnosis) and in
    Judaism (Kabbala). Moreover, it is important to study more care-
    fully the influence of Neo-Platonism on the Renaissance and nu-
    merous mystico-occult trends (from Bruno to the Rosicrucians
    and Hermetics).

10. The significance of Neo-Platonism is fundamentally understated
    in contemporary Orthodoxy. Intellectualism is not the sole path
    of the Christian, but the absence of intellect, or systematic, emo-
    tional weak-mindedness and blind devotionalism, are not likely,
    for their part, to be the correct paths. Not everyone understands
    Christian doctrine deeply. Neo-Platonic philosophy can help us
    understand it better.

7.

HERACLITUS AND CONTEMPORARY RUSSIA

Theses Towards the Modernization of Russian Society

1. Western philosophy began with Heraclitus and his teaching concerning logos. Heidegger shows that it also ended with him. Hegel and Nietzsche, who completed Western philosophy, gave special attention to precisely Heraclitus.

2. Russian philosophy has not begun at all. What there was, was only the first efforts to think philosophically, which slipped away. Logos in its European understanding is clearly not Russia's lot. Chaos is our lot. But…

3. We saw (in previous seminars) that chaos is not the exclusion of logos, but its *inclusion*. Logos is in chaos. The chaos that does not have logos WITHIN it is a rubbish heap, the archeomodern, not chaos. Chaos is teeming; it is always pregnant.

4. There must be Logos in Russian chaos. It got mixed up in chaos's folds. If [that which is] Russian [*russkoe*] is chaos, and not a

rubbish heap, then *logos must definitely be there*. It can be helped out, but no one — no one! — can or should force us to repeat the path of the radical severance of logos from chaos (as happened in Western European philosophy). We can allow that we will share *the structure of the moment of the appearance of logos from chaos* with Western European philosophy, but everything else will most likely be completely different, all the more so the end, which there cannot be at all in a philosophy of chaos.

5. Continuing the hypothesis: Russian philosophy should begin with Heraclitus, but it is not yet a fact that it must make the same subsequent steps as Western philosophy did. That is not even the most important thing. Let's BEGIN with Heraclitus. That is enough. If that proves possible, it will be a BEGINNING.

6. Already from the first fragment, and you can read him from any fragment, Heraclitus calls us to the Logos (*to sophon*), to another. "Listening not to me but to the logos, all is one." Russians at once seize upon "all is one," and they forget that it is necessary to listen not to oneself, or Heraclitus, but *the logos*. For Russians, in our chaos, all is one as it is, without Heraclitus. That is what the logos dissolved in chaos says (Vladimir Solovyov's all-unity), but in this way we won't go far into philosophy. The way we understand that "all is one" is nonsense. We must start from the fact that Heraclitus himself did not understand that all is one, but understood that all is diverse and separate and does not gather together. That is, Heraclitus divided everything. And in order to stop dividing it, he had to be struck by the incursion of the logos, hit by lightning. Here Russians cease to understand anything: "What lightning? Everything is already clear to us: all is one. Of course it is one…" You see how everything is neglected… Before Heraclitus, it had to be explained to us that *all is not one*. Russians lack a psychological

foundation for philosophy. The force of chaos is too strong in us. That is very good, but while that is so, we will not find logos in our Russian folds.

7. One must eradicate Solovyov from oneself and become, at least for a while, a bit saner. *Around us is a multitude.* Whoever does not admit this now loses his audience. Not with shame, but with *honor,* the Russian narod [i.e. people] thinks, and thinks correctly, but then it doesn't need Heraclitus: it already knows everything. It doesn't even need Solovyov. The Russian narod is just fine by itself. But in its natural state the Russian narod does not want to look for logos, won't start looking for it, and never looked for it earnestly. What does it need a part of chaos for, an infinitely small part, at that?! It is all of chaos at once — the richer choice. The narod does not miscalculate, but there can be no philosophy under these circumstances until something changes.

8. Heraclitus is *the limit of complexity* for a Russian. The lack of un-derstanding of him blocks us here and now from philosophy as such, both far Western and Eastern (religious, Hindu, Chinese), and from the possibility of creating an original philosophy. Until we inquire into Heraclitus, at least his first fragments, but also all the rest, we stand firmly in place, i.e. we sleep.

9. The search for the logos consists of *two steps.* The first step: to leave enchanted sleep and establish wakefulness in the world of *multiplicity.* That is painful. It is almost unbearable. It is entirely not the [usual] Russian way. When Russians apprehend it, they curse. Russians have no givens for that: not in culture, not in education, not in psychology. But without that, everything else is debarred. As carriers of chaos, Russians are *magical*; to under-stand that the world is manifold, they must become *ordinary.* They must disenchant themselves. That is exceedingly unpleasant

to do. It is possible only *outside* chaos. It is necessary to come out of chaos — not into order, but into the space of pain, or more likely into disorder.

10. The second step: it is necessary *to be consumed in the rays of the vertical axis* that pierces the human who is gazing perplexedly at the surrounding multiplicity. The axis is fire and lightning. "Pur" (fire) and "keraunos" (lightning) are two names of being in Heraclitus, but they hit only one place: the field of tension *between* the vigilant human and the multiplicity that oppresses him. If something is lacking — the human, the oppression, or the multiplicity — *the fire won't have a place.* The lightning will have nowhere to strike. Lightning only strikes *outside chaos.* There, outside chaos, is also where all Heraclitus' formulas come to-gether: there is discovered phusis, aeon, gods, and people, "ethos anthropo daimon," Zeus, which "to sophon" loves and does not love to be called, etc.

11. *Outside* chaos, the majestic architecture of order is built. Order is a construct stretched out around lightning and fire, around the logos. That is how the space of philosophy is created. For this we must go *outside* (from a philosophical perspective, we live in the center of the earth, under the earth; our skies and luminaries are artificial; it is a hollow earth, mother-earth, earth-water, earth of the abyss, liquid earth) and from without become worthy [*spodo-bytsya*] of the strike. There along the axis of lightning will be hierarchies, ranks, levels, ladders and orders; there is height and depth there. They are one and the same, according to Heraclitus, because for residents of chaos there is neither one nor the other, and when height appears, depth does, too. Humans and gods dwell there, and also animals and spirits. There. That is impor-tant: THERE. That is, *not here.*

12. Western European philosophy, which found itself on the outside and lightning-struck, remained captivated by the majestic edifice of logos for centuries, and it was spoiled *there*. Logos initially pulsated, then cooled, then froze and withered. Then it split into myriad remains. Each Western European person got a piece, like rock from the Berlin wall. That is his personal logos — more precisely, what remains of it. It is no longer living and is a relic. Logos dissipated among lost multitudes is the society of the rubbish heap (contemporary Western postmodernity). According to Heidegger, such a world should either start from the beginning (another Beginning) or vanish. All of that does not concern us: we have not yet seriously begun a first time.

13. We have other problems. I described two steps. The third step consists in *recognizing chaos in logos*, in seeing that the same is outside as inside. We must see in foreign logos native [*rodimyy*] chaos and *make logos native*. We must not go the path of Icarus; we must return to the lowlands, along the path of Orpheus (it is possible that we must turn and look at what they did with Eurydice…); return, but illuminated by light, pierced by fire, consumed by lightning. Only then will we be able to understand the secret dimension of Heraclitus the Dark: all is one — *logos is chaos*. Darkness is light. THERE is here.

14. Westerners did not understand Heraclitus. They thought that "all is one" applies ONLY to what is outside. They forgot the breath of the abyss they climbed out of, the smell of raw non-being. "All" for them is only the vertical of illumination and the horizontal of the commonplace. "All" for us is that which is on the outside, the place where lightning strikes, but also that which sleeps in the depths of the earth, pretending to be the Russian narod.

15. Heraclitus is an ethnic Russian philosopher, or rather he can become one, if we take the three steps.

16. The teaching of philosophy in Russia should begin and end with Heraclitus. Until we develop a *Russian* relation to him, until we understand him, the way forward is harmful and lacking for us.

17. That is the first (and last) law of modernization.

8.

A CONVERSATION ABOUT NOOMACHY

Natella Speranskaya: In the five-volume work *Noomachy*, you develop the themes of *In Search of the Dark Logos* where you first present the model of three Logoi, three intellectual worlds, to which you gave names of Greek gods: Apollo, Dionysus, and Cybele. Your new book is called *Noomachy* (Wars of the Intellect), which refers us back to Heraclitus' Polemos (Πόλεμος), and also to the Titanomachia (Τιτανομαχία) and Gigantomachia (Γιγαντομαχία), found at the center of attention of a number of ancient authors (Hesiod, Homer, Apollodorus, Ovid, Sophocles, etc.). Please tell us about this concept.

Alexander Dugin: To tell you about it is the same as to give a brief account of the content of all five volumes and *In Search of the Dark Logos*. You ask me to do something beyond my strength. But I'll try to do it as briefly as possible. At some moment, I became keenly interested in the problem of the pluralism of types of consciousness. This is the basic idea of Eurasianism: the plurality of civilizations and the baselessness of the Western pretension to universalism. Alain de Benoist affirms the same thing in his theory of the pluriverse and critique of Eurocentrism. The plural anthropology of Boas and Levi-Strauss also applies here. Accepting the thesis that structures of rationality can be organized differently in different cultures, I tried to develop my own model, which would systematize more general types of rationality.

I began by trying to discover an alternative to the system of rationality that is regarded as classical and stems from Greco-Roman antiquity. Following Nietzsche, I called this the Logos of Apollo. From there, I tried to determine the structures of an alternative rationality that I again following Nietzsche called the Logos of Dionysus. *In Search of the Dark Logos* was dedicated to clarifying the structure of Dionysus. Initially I thought that two Logoi, i.e. two types of rationality, would be enough for the basic model of the plurality of structures of consciousness. But the more I studied the dualism of Apollo/Dionysus, the exclusive/inclusive, I came to the conclusion, empirically and phenomenologically, that this pair does not cover all types of rationality and that another absolutely distinct fundamental structure could be detected: the Logos of Cybele. So Dionysus transformed from the black Logos to the dark Logos; his secret color was discovered against the backdrop of Cybele's darkness. That is how I came to the idea of three Logoi, on which *Noomachy* is based.

In developing this theme, I constructed a noology (a term first used by the Romanian philosopher Lucian Blaga) based on a cartography of the three types of rationality: Apollonian, Dionysian, and Cybelean. Each of them corresponds to a distinct and irreducible paradigmal structure, which is not an idea-variant [*neideovariativnaya*], capable of unfolding into an indeterminately large number of mythologies, philosophies, religions, theologies, scientific disciplines, or styles of art. This paradigmal structure is the Logos. Neo-Platonists (Plotinus in particular) saw the concretization of Nous in Logos. If we accept my model, we get not one concretization but three. These are three camps found in essential, irremovable enmity, in opposition. At the same time, the three Logoi allow us to move away from the direct opposition of Apollo/Dionysus taken from Nietzsche and to get a much more complex and detailed picture. Moreover, asymmetrical alliances are possible among the Logoi: Indo-European culture is based on the union of Apollo and Dionysus. The Semitic world opposes to this an alliance of the black double of Apollo, Titan, with Cybele, the Great Mother, though in the context of inner opposition within the limits of the matriarchal, Androgynate Agdistis. And in the five volumes of *Noomachy*, I study all these correspondences, interweavings, superimpositions, and differentiations of layers, as well as a triple model of basic hermeneutics (each thing, each word, each narrative thus implies the possibility of a triple reading depending on which Logos we choose as our starting point). The first volume is a general introduction to the three Logoi and an analysis of their connections with the three groups of philosophical schools in ancient Greece. Then I move to a more detailed examination of the influence of the Logoi in concrete civilizations, where the proportion and balance is different each time, while histories and historials give this balance an additional dynamic component. The body of *Noomachy* took shape as a result of these noological studies. It is most likely a preliminary survey, a sort of broad introduction to the problematic. After writing five volumes, I realized that that was only a table of contents, each part of which contains myriad semantic universes. Thus, *Noomachy* is an open project. First, we all participate in it. Second, we can do so thoughtfully and consciously.

The prospects are exciting, but to understand what I have in mind, it is first necessary to read, and as much as possible, to gain an understanding of the content of the five volumes. After that, many things will become clear, but others, by contrast, will prove dark as night.

NS: In 1900, Merezhkovsky called Nietzsche a great European philosopher who managed to resurrect "two Olympian gods, Apollo and Dionysus, in the old European graveyard." A hundred years later, another great philosopher discovers the three Logoi, resurrecting the names Dionysus, Apollo, and Cybele, thereby producing a universal key to the enigram of all philosophical and religious teachings, domains of knowledge, and civilizational paradigms. In this way, the very approach to the interpretation of any phenomena, systems, symbols, etc., changes fundamentally, and today the "revaluation of all values" will mean nothing other than the revaluation of the reigning values of the contemporary world through comprehension of the predominant type of interpretation. Is it possible to say for sure which type of interpretation, which picture of the world (Apollonian, Dionysian, Cybelean), predominates today, and if it is possible, what system of values this predominant view offers?

AD: Three Logoi is not simply two + one. It is not the mechanical addition to Apollo and Dionysus of one more figure. It is something much more important and profound. Nietzsche's dual topos, genius in itself, from which I began and without which there wouldn't even be the possibility of approach to the theme of three Logoi, conceals a fundamental difference between Dionysus and Cybele, which does not allow us to correctly diagnose our time, and more precisely, the contemporary [*kontemporal'nomu*] condition of modern [*sovremennoy*] European and Eurocentric civilization. And the diagnosis is: the complete predominance of the Great Mother, Cybele. Cybele today reigns supreme [absolutely, sovereignly; *polnovlastno*, with full power]. That is the most dramatic thing in Noomachy: we are dealing not with Dionysus, who replaces the Apollo of classical rationality. We are dealing with Titans and the reign of quantity (Guénon), with the Empire of Matter. This matter has its own Logos, setting out interpretational paradigms that predetermine the essence of modernity and postmodernity, and instead of Dionysus, his black counterpart, Adonis, acts here. This is Dionysus's double, his titanic simulacrum. At the same time, the astonishing thing is that Europe's essence is the

Logos of Apollo in union with Dionysus. The fact that Cybele rules today means the following: we are dealing not with Europe, but with anti-Europe. But what is Europe? Does it still exist? Yes, but it must be sought in the zone of other Logoi. To break through to it, it is necessary once again to overcome the Great Mother, to defeat and overthrow the rebellious Titans in Tartarus, i.e. to win Noomachy. After all, precisely that was the start of Indo-European civilization, and in particular, Greco-Roman Mediterranean culture. We have to either say goodbye to Europe, or begin Europe anew. That could be another approach to what Heidegger called "Another Beginning." We can call it the "return of Apollo" or "the final epiphany of Dionysus," "the Dionysus of the Dawn, without which the return of Apollo will not occur."

NS: In a seminar on Heraclitus, Heidegger's student Eugene Fink talks about how the Greeks represent a massive challenge for us, and, despite the fact that the voice of Heraclitus of Ephesus, like the voice of the Pythia, reaches us through a thousand years, we still have not reached Heraclitus himself. In this first volume of *Noomachy*, you write about the necessity for distance from the "contemporary moment," since only that will allow us to delineate the structure of the "historial" and to immerse ourselves in the life world of one or another philosopher. This seems rather difficult to do, especially concerning the removal of Eurocentricity. This, after all, entails nothing else than the intellectual practice of delineating the philosophical slice (and proto-philosophical) of already not one civilization (Western), but many civilizations, each with its own Logos. In order to grasp Heraclitus, we must "become Heraclitus," but to the same extent, we must also become Suhrawardi, Avicenna, Nagarjuna, Nichiren, and others. How can a contemporary thinker attain the necessary distance and become absolutely open for the understanding of various schools and tendencies of thought? Does a sort of "map" of civilizations exist that brings to light Logoi different from the Logos of Western European philosophy, the end of which was established long ago?

AD: Therein lies the difficulty. We are not free from our historial, since precisely it predetermines our content, and hence the structures of the Logos that form us. Distance is impossible if we make it an end in itself; we will only arrive at a serpentine twist of ourselves, like moving around the Mobius strip. We must become Heraclitus, but it is not possible to do so. We can try to become a Greek and try even harder to become an ancient Greek. There is no guarantee, but the very desire to emigrate from out of the present is highly important. The construction of a map of civilizations is intended to give at least a few reference points for how to make that distance real. And as I have already said, getting out from under the hypnosis of contemporary (and post-contemporary) European rationality will already show to what extent contemporary Europe in its structure is noologically far from, or even directly opposed to, Europe as such. The postmodernists that brought down the structures understood this clearly: the European logos is in fact in radical opposition to the contemporary European moment. If we are carriers of European identity, then we are in the Titans' captivity, sold into slavery to them. If we do not experience the West as decline, we are shadows of the Titans, which means that we are not autochthonous Europeans, but noological immigrants, nomads, eroding European structures once and for all (the precise meaning of the concept of poststructuralism). The map of civilizations outlines the circle of the European Logos, its frontier regions and the zones that don't depend on it. Thereby there emerges a synchronous map of frozen time distributed along semantic axes. Theoretically, this should open the possibility for the practice of a philosophy of distance, placing the moments (including the contemporary) into the historial, and the historial into the more general field of noological structures. Thus, Noomachy appears before us in many slices, temporal and spatial, and each civilization has its own unique proportions of balance of Logoi, congealed into dynamic crystals of semantic types. Time is a sequence of meanings. If we understand the meaning of time, we acquire a special noetic life where contemporaneity and even the limits of a civilization cease to be fatal. That is the original meaning of the term theoria (θεωρία) as interpreted by Festugière in the spirit of Platonic and pre-Platonic philosophy. Contemplating what is diverse in its structures, a thinker reaches the semantic core, and then begins to contemplate that very core. The three Logoi are the structure of the core, and concentrated attention on it allows one to comprehend the plurality of civilizations in their uniqueness and unicity, since in each civilization the Logoi always fight among themselves in a manner intrinsic only to that civilization.

NS: Referring to Julius Evola's well-known work *Ride the Tiger*, you talk about the fact that it is possible to view the contemporary world ("contemporary moment") and Tradition as co-existing synchronously. which means that we should be able to find traces of the contemporary in even earlier stages, correct? I remember that when I paid close attention to the observation of another traditionalist, René Guénon, he said the sources of the contemporary world should be sought in classical antiquity. I immersed myself in the heritage of the epic poets, early mythographers, and pre-Socratic thinkers, and established that even the legendary "Seven Sages" prepared what today we call "the end of philosophy." Moreover, I discovered with surprise that various schools and tendencies of thought, and also separate thinkers, were under the influence of one of the three (synchronously existing in space) Logoi: Apollo, Dionysus, and Cybele. This co-existence was not peaceful. On the contrary, all three Logoi were in a state of tense battle (which you call Noomachy). The final collapse of the original union of Dionysus and Apollo led to the total domination of the Cybelean Logos. Guénon was absolutely right: he guessed clearly that traces of the contemporary world were already present in this period. Can we assume that the opposite is also the case: traces of Tradition can still be found in the contemporary [world]? If Tradition continues to co-exist with contemporaneity, should we expect the turning of the hourglass? Who will turn it: the human, as the one found "between" (the contemporary and Tradition), or is this radical gesture beyond man's power and someone else needed?

AD: Concerning the contemporaneity [contemporary character] of the thought of the pre-Socratics and especially of Democritus and Epicurus: that is entirely accurate. The same is true in general of the substantialist and proto-material pursuits of the early natural philosophers, where the shadow of the contemporary [world] is fully discernible. In some sense the materialism of modernity consisted in a rediscovery of pre-Socratic atomism and a number of Epicurean doctrines, through Lucretius in particular. That is, Tradition and the contemporary should be understood synchronously, as types of philosophy, culture, and society. Apollo and Dionysus rule over Tradition; Cybele and the Titans [rule over] the contemporary. There is a battle between Tradition and the contemporary, and that is Noomachy. The battle is eternal. Apollo and Dionysus (Tradition) won the main victory in it, but Cybele and the Titans sometimes have tactical successes. The contemporary, modernity, is the epoch of the temporary triumph of the Titans and the Great Mother, Cybele. Apollo and Dionysus were forced to retreat; matter became humanity's master. This began with the West, the countries where the sun sets. According to Heidegger, we are on the cusp of the Great Midnight. The contemporary predominates and does not even understand that there can be something other than itself, but there is something other than it. Tradition, and the returning solar gods. In the Great Midnight the turn that you are asking about occurs. Who accomplishes it? That question is central in the philosophy of Heidegger's middle period. He resolves it in a complicated manner: through Ereignis on the side of authentically existing Dasein and through the appearance, passing by, of the "last God" (*letzte Gott*). But both members of the pair Dasein — last God have, and do not have, a relation to the human. In some sense, Dasein is the core of human [adj.], and the *letzte Gott* is that which appears to Dasein from the side of the Fourfold (*Geviert*) opposite to humanity. This moment is the moment of turning [*perevorot*]. The human [adj.] should only be thought of as paired. Thus, Dionysus lives inside Apollo. Both these elements are present in Socrates. Plato is strictly Apollonian. But if that is so, the alliance of the two main figures of Indo-European culture is open to him, and he praises their unity and their harmony, delighting in his teacher Socrates in the most diverse situations that reveal now one, now another side of this perfect human.

NS: Who was Socrates's daimon, which never impelled him to do anything, but only cautioned the philosopher against doing anything wrong?

AD: In contemporary Iran there is a Council of Spiritual Expediency [Expediency Discernment Council]. It consists of spiritual authorities, Ayatollahs, it plays an important role in State rule. It also does not impel [anyone] toward anything, that's what President and parliament are for, but cautions against wrong acts. Socrates's daimon is a form of the paradigmatic presence that is not the rational and voluntary ego (it does not impel), but illuminates with a momentary flash the context of each concrete problematic. A person's "I" is martial, but Socrates's daimon is priestly. It knows what truth is, while Socrates himself, being a partial occurrence inside his daimon, cannot know that. The daimon keeps an eye on "spiritual expediency." It does not act for Socrates; it subtly looks after him. But in contrast to bodily-oriented persons, Socrates's daimon is a luminous, Apollonian cone based in the bright sky. Socrates himself is a divine and daimonic person. Titanic man is philistine, and his ego rests on a cone whose foundations lie deep in the earth. This sort of person is titanic and cybelean. Socrates's daimon stands higher than him. The titanic self of the material person is ruled by another, non-spiritual expediency, inlaying the individual in the folds of material darkness.

NS: The issue about how the question of matter was resolved in antiquity seems to me extremely important. And how, in accordance with the triadic model of Logoi, do you resolve it in *Noomachy*? In the chapter on Cybele, you present twenty principles of black philosophy, giving precisely matter the predominant place.

AD: Matter is etymologically like the Greek hyle (ὕλη), timber. That is an Aristotelian term. Semantically it means the lower limit of bodily forms, that which is lower than the elements from out of which corporeality is woven. The tree is the symbol of the Great Mother. The tree is the trick of an optic-ontological illusion: it seems to the observer that it grows from the Earth, which produces it from itself. But the tree grows from the seed, not from the Earth. Consciousness of the role of the seed is the beginning of patriarchal philosophy, the cult of the Father and Son. Earth is important, but it does not give things being. Earth in a philosophical sense is sterile; it is the milieu, but not the bearing impulse. It does not give things being; it accepts a small being (seed) and helps it have its fill of juices, feeds it (the wet-nurse-*Khôra* in *Timaeus*). That is a solar relation to matter, which itself does not exist (like the seed exists) and does not give things being. But in matriarchal cultures, among "peoples of the sea," and certain Western Semites there is the idea of the birth-giving Earth, i.e. matter as possessing being and granting being. This being of the earth is embodied in the tree, in timber. The tree is a seal (of the imagined, for Indo-Europeans) being of Earth. That is the woods, hyle (ὕλη), and the Latin *materia*, matter. The optico-ontological illusion of the tree is a [*praistok*[1]] of materialism and black philosophy, which understands the world from below and explains the higher through the lower. In antiquity, this understanding was characteristic of Western Semitic cultures, the Phoenicians in particular, and it is possible that it passed from them to the Hellenic pre-Socratics, and later to the Stoics, as Pohlenz and Sidash show. The Great Mother — wood [tree] — matter. That is the chain of homologies leading from myth to philosophy. But one can move along it in the opposite direction also. Then any, even the most nuanced materialism, will be a variant of the cult of the Great Mother.

NS: My next question is similar to the previous one, but this time I would like to ask you about the place of evil in the picture of the three Logoi.

AD: That is a huge topic. Apollo knows evil as being's depleted (depleting) antithesis. If day exists, night does not exist. But if clouds cover the sky, the sun will come out sooner or later. Night still does not exist, since there is day and the sun of day. Apollo refers evil back to evil, night to night, and with disgust he tells chthonic Python, cast down by him, "continue to rot" (πύθω). Dionysus knows the game of good/evil, this/other. He is non-dually dual. He suffers, lacerated by the Titans, but he plays with them and battles simultaneously. Evil for Dionysus is always relative. He is always ready to turn the proportions around. He is not beyond morality; he bears a certain Dionysian morality, the morality of epiphany, the morality of Presence. Cybele regards evil as a light that falls on her, consumes her, stings her, and shows the frightful picture of her face. Cybele lives by night and darkness, and in the best case by the swampy fires of St. Elmo. In its malleable embrace there is no opposition of good/evil. A mother forgives and loves all

---

1 *pra* = "pre", *istok* = "source" or "origin". So, the illusion of the tree is the pre-origin of materialism. — Tn.

her progeny, both the saints and the sinners, both the virtuous and the vicious. Cybele is truly amoral and only hates the blue lucidity of the heavens, in which it reads its condemnation. Flight upward, without a return downward, is for Cybele the sum of all evil. To take flight and not fall, not return into the depths of the Earth — that is unbearable for Cybele. That is why Cybele loves fights but hates war: in war, the hero is capable of ascending to the heavens and thus avoiding its grasp.

NS: Over what does Plotinus fundamentally disagree with the Gnostics and why do you think that "Gnosticism is the childhood disease of Platonism"?

AD: Plotinus is a purely Apollonian philosopher. He does not understand the tragic element of the Gnostics. Yes, the ingress of souls into the vice of matter is, for Plotinus, an extremely unpleasant episode of fate, but he does not give that condition the metaphysical meaning that the Gnostics give it. Plotinus thinks that the Gnostics hold on to their ego too tenaciously, causing them to suffer. A person can be caught in the snare of matter, but if he closes his eyes and contemplates the ideas, this difficulty will be forgotten and will disappear. Within lives the soul, and if someone looks at it steadfastly, at some point it will look back in return. When the soul looks at the ego, it abolishes material chimeras and opens the horizons of the Intellect. The world is a copy, Plotinus agrees with the Gnostics, but it is not such a bad copy. The charms of the Great Mother do not reach Plotinus. He does not understand the inescapability of the material burden. The philosophical gesture of turning the head towards the opposite direction (the Platonic cave in the *Republic*) comes to him easily and like a man. And he is ready to raise himself up, and he does not give meaning to the howls and spasms of matter. He is completely free of the female principle, whereas the Gnostics are not.

NS: In his work on the life of Plotinus, Porphyry cites the well-known legend that in response to Amelius' invitation to participate in a rite associated with the full moon, his teacher Plotinus said, "the gods should come to me, and not I to them." Many students were confused about how to interpret Plotinus's words, and some even accused him of disdaining the traditional cults. Pierre Hadot sees in Plotinus's words the indication of a peculiar understanding of divine presence. He writes, "to find God, it is not necessary to go to His temples. It is not necessary to go anywhere to find His presence. But one must oneself become a living temple, where it could manifest." What do you think of Hadot's interpretation and how do you understand Plotinus's words about the gods?

AD: The worship of God is not in the body, but in the soul. In the context of spiritual geography, this is one of the most important themes of our Gospel. In particular, in the Gospel of John, in the conversation with the Samaritan who asks where one must worship God: "Jesus tells her, believe Me, a time is coming when you will worship the Father neither on this mountain nor in Jerusalem." That is a specific time, which is the time of the Soul. In my opinion, Plotinus means sometimes similar. There are external rituals and there are internal ones. The philosopher is located under the direct ray of eidetic presence, and wherever he might be, this ray is with him, and it pierces him each time he begins to think, but for Plotinus, the element of thought is divine. The highest ideas are gods and he who is able to contemplate them is in direct association with God. In the Christian tradition this has another interpretation, but the meaning of the superiority of the inner to the outer is the same. In the traditions of radical Shiism, Ismailism, the call to a radical opposition of the inner over the outer was given even more drastic forms, right up to the abrogation of Islamic regulations among the Qarmatians, or in the time of the announcement of the era of spiritual renaissance at the Alamut Castle. I've written about these events in the third volume of *Noomachy*.

NS: You talk about the female nature of the demiurge, indicating thereby its belonging to the "black" Logos of Cybele. Nevertheless, when determining the place of Gnosticism in the three noetic universes, you locate it in the zone of the Logos of Dionysus, a Logos found dangerously close to the Logos of Cybele. Which secrets of the Great Mother does Gnosticism begin to open? Talk about the role of the "female creator" in *Noomachy*.

AD: The Gnostic worldview is very complex. Any attempt to reject or accept it at the outset seems superficial to me. A Gnostic is the bearer of the unhappy consciousness, but according to Hegel only the unhappy consciousness is capable of philosophy. The happy consciousness is a dream, and at the limit, the absence of consciousness altogether. The world of the Gnostics is dual and problematic. That is why it relates to the zone of Dionysus, where duality reigns. The Gnostic is not an acolyte of Cybele, but in contrast to patriarchal Apollonianism, he feels himself captive to Her. He knows the might of the Great Mother, and guesses the secret of the titanic usurpation of the Female Creator [*Tvorchika*], who poses as the creating Father, while being in fact a usurper, a female androgyne [sic]. The Gnostic exposes the ontological illusiveness of the corporeal world, but he cannot yet deal with this illusiveness. He is a hero tortured and tormented by matter. His drama is the drama of Dionysus. The Gnostic is torn apart by Titans and rises above them in fierce battle with the Great Mother. The Gnostic knows the entire titanic principle, since Titan is the matrix of the human, his extended (downward) chthonic and hypochthonic foundation. The Gnostic carries the abyss in himself. He knows the Great Mother as his I, which he strives to overcome, as the spirit of gravity. The Gnostic is Dionysus in the role of Adonis, trying to quit the field of the black game of self-delighting, infernal femininity. Recognizing that the creator of the world is a woman, the Gnostic rushes to that in relation to which Sophia is a woman, i.e. in the world of the Pleroma, to the apophatic, ineffable Father, concealed by a veil of black material marvels. That is a very subtle move: the Gnostic does not accept the Great Mother as an answer; he spiritualizes her as a question, co-suffers [empathizes with] its drama, theopathically lives the mystery of her insurrection and the revolution of the aeons, which is reflected in myths about Sophia, in particular in the teachings of Valentinus.

NS: You say that in describing the war of the Athenians with the Atlantids, Proclus in fact describes the battle of two Logoi (the Logos of Apollo and the Logos of Cybele). In the same way, do you think it is possible to view certain historical events in the context of noetic battles? Athens against Atlantis. Rome against Carthage. The primeval duel between Land and Sea. The furious clash of the Olympian heroic principle with the Titans of the Great Mother. Can we say that the application of the model of the three Logoi, in attempting to explain historical processes, will mean nothing other than contact with hiero-history, "sacred history"?

AD: Precisely so. In polemics with me, some contemporary tradition-alists insist that geopolitics is not a sacred science but is fully exhausted by profane, modernistic considerations in the spirit of strategic studies or political analysis. The example of Proclus disproves that opinion. Geopolitics is built on the comprehension of qualitative space, which lies at the basis of sacred geography. We can say that geopolitics is a simplified and rationalized version of sacred geography. The entire structure of Ishraq philosophy, analyzed by Corbin in particular, is based on this metaphysical understanding of space. Yes, the academic version of geopolitics is entirely rational and scientific, but it is easy to recognize deeper roots at its basis, which, by the way, is easy to see in my early book *Foundations of Geopolitics*, where there is a chapter called "From Sacred Geography to Geopolitics." In Proclus's interpretation of the history of Atlantis, given in the beginning of the *Timaeus*, we see precisely an example of "sacred geopolitics." I think that the symbols and models used by Plato, and interpreted by Proclus, in relation to the Atlantids and Athenians, describes with perfect precision the basic characteristics of thalassocracy on one hand and telurocracy on the other. In our time these symbols and signs are still recognizable and intelligible, right up to the Pillars of Hercules on the dollar bill, with the reversed motto *Plus Ultra* instead of *Nec Plus Ultra*. Passing beyond the Western limit of the Mediterranean, Indo-European culture enters the phase of hubris (ὕβρις), i.e. it violates measure and falls under the influence of the Logos of Cybele and the elements of titanism. That is exactly what happened in Europe beginning in the 17th century and ending in the establishment of a New Babylon in the US. An analysis based on the three Logoi is indeed fully relevant for the analysis of contemporary events and processes in a hiero-historical perspective.

NS: In his book *Against the Modern World: Traditionalism and the Secret Intellectual History of the Twentieth Century*, Mark Sedgwick notes that the origins of traditionalism should be sought in Renaissance-era Italy, i.e. the era when, according to Guénon, an inversion of traditional wisdom occurred. Essentially, traditionalism was a reaction and answer to this inversion. Sedgwick calls the eminent Italian thinker, Marsilio Ficino, one of the predecessors of traditionalism. Ficino translated the *Corpus Hermeticum*, regarding it as an ancient expression of the Perennial Philosophy, Philosophia Perennis. However, as Isaac Casaubon and later Frances Yates showed (see *Giordano Bruno and the Hermetic Tradition*), the texts ascribed to Hermes Trismegistus were written, not in pre-Christian antiquity, but in the 2nd-3rd centuries of the common era. In approximately 1460, as Yates writes, a Greek manuscript came from Macedonia to Florence containing the list of the *Corpus Hermeticum* (excluding the last, fifteenth tract). Although earlier Cosimo de' Medici gave Ficino the directive to translate the texts of the great Plato, the sudden appearance of works of Thrice-Great Hermes forced him to set aside the translation of Platonic texts. He asked Ficino to urgently translate the Hermetic *Corpus*. "From the Church fathers Cosimo and Ficino knew that Hermes Trismegistus is much older than Plato," Yates writes.

> They also knew the Latin 'Asclepius,' who kindled the thirst for ancient Egyptian wisdom from that same original source. Egypt is older than Greece; Hermes is older than Plato. The Renaissance honored everything old and original as standing closer to the divine truth. Accordingly, the Hermetic *Corpus* had to be translated before Plato's *Republic* or *Symposium*. That is why that project became Ficino's first translation.

At that time, no one entertained the thought of chronological error. The *Corpus Hermeticum*, a post-Christian text, proved to be at the center of the rebirth of magic in the Renaissance era, and is also regarded as an authentic and ancient expression of Philosophia Perennis. The Vedic texts (whose wisdom was adopted by the traditionalists of the 20th century, and also by their predecessors, like Reuben Barrow in the 18th century) could not have been the source of traditionalism in the Renaissance because the thinkers of that period couldn't have known them. One can ask why the thinkers of the Renaissance era did not look for the origins of Perennial Philosophy in the wisdom of earlier, ancient philosophers, especially in the fundamental problematic of Titano- and Gigantomachy, but put their entire interest in the early (pre-Socratic, as we can say now) ancient philosophy focused on Epicureanism (Lorenzo Valla's attention to the philosophy of Epicurus and Lucretius, and, in consequence, his essay "On Pleasure") and the atomism of Democritus (which gets its "second life" precisely at that time).

AD: Lorenzo Valla is not the entire Renaissance. The Florentine Academy discovered Platonism and Neo-Platonism, as well as Hermeticism, as you noted. Precisely that was the most striking moment of the Renaissance. In my opinion, Philosophia Perennis can very well be regarded as broadly understood Platonism and, to an even greater extent, Neo-Platonism. There are many parallels here to the Vedas and other forms of traditional metaphysics, but for Western European thought, Platonism fits optimally. Pure Platonism is pure Apollonianism: it has no room for Titanomachy only because it has no room for Titans. Plato completely defeats and destroys the Titans. In Neo-Platonism one can see a certain element of struggle, but it is removed by a vertical dash into the sphere of the transcendent, which removes the tension of the battle and makes philosophy more of a game. This is victorious Dionysus abstracted from his passionate, theopathic side, hence the Renaissance's increased attention to the game. At the same time hermeticism blossomed, in which there are many subjects similar to Titanomachy. This hermeticism could have both a purely Dionysian nature or a Cybelean one, where we approach the theme of "black alchemy," and, accordingly, atomism, Epicurus, and Lucretius, but, to repeat, that is just one of the possibilities of the Renaissance, alongside the Apollo and Dionysus of the Florentine Platonists. As for the pre-Socratics, they were for a long time part of general hermetic discourse, and reference to them (most often apocryphal) was typical of a certain sort of alchemical literature, for instance, in one of the oldest texts of the *Turba Philosophorum*.

NS: Your teacher Yevgeny Golovin said that in the Renaissance and Modernity, the so-called "magic of black water" (*aqua nigra, sal nibri*) flourished. One of the aims of this was to receive "black lunar magnesium," which was regarded as the infernal counterpart to the lapis philosophorum. That substance was capable of transforming ordinary metals into pure silver or gold. At issue, if I understand correctly, is what can be called "black alchemy." Appealing to Bonardel's investigations, you distinguish "negative alchemy," which is found under the sign of the Titan Prometheus. Accordingly, this alchemy can be called titanic, the "black alchemy" of the Great Mother, Cybele. In contrast to Hermetic alchemy, this alchemy works with natural substances and prioritizes the zone of the Earth and underground world. According to Bonardel, the Hermetic art moved under the sign of Prometheus in the Renaissance era. That was when, in Golovin's words, the "magic of black water" flourished. Who are they, these adepts of "black Hermeticism"? What forms did Noomachy take in the period when the difference between two types of Hermetic art became clear?

AD: The most frightful adepts of "black magnesia" are modern scientists [the scientists of the modern era], who built their concepts on a scientific picture of the world. The black magic and alchemy of the Renaissance are children compared to modern physics, chemistry, or biology. At the end of the Middle Ages, the process of placing being in matter (atomism, the hylozoism of Bernardino Telesio, Gassendi, or Spinoza) was just beginning; that was the "attraction of black magnesium." Material operations and interpretations of doctrines and alchemical practices began to prevail in the context of the Hermetic *Corpus*, later leading to modern chemistry. The scientific picture of the world, representing the cosmic of Cybele, was formed on their basis. Plato's ideas disappeared beyond the horizon, and Aristotle's eidoi were reduced to eidolons and then to "black water," i.e. to matter and its vortices. Modern science is well-organized Satanism, operating with that which, in the world, is the most chimerical, illusionary, and infernal, a collection of material bodies, atoms, and particles, disappearing into the matrix of the lord-mother, and emerging therefrom, only to disappear again. Eliade said something similar when he spoke of the origins of modern European science and its connections with hermeticism (in the book *Aspects du Mythe*, if I recall correctly).

NS: We have become used to the concept of the androgyne, the male-female divinity, from the perspective of the Logos of Dionysus, i.e. as the combination of the male and female principles. In *Noomachy*, you explain in detail that there is another perspective on the androgyne, from the position of Apollo and from the position of Cybele. What is the main difference in these perspectives? Don't you think that Plato was the one who was able to realize the Apollonian androgyne?

AD: Yes, the androgyne is interpreted in accordance with the pre-dominance of one or another Logos. In the Apollonian androgyne, the female principle is entirely subsumed by the male. Its example is Pallas Athena, in whom almost absolute masculinity is embodied. Beginning from birth — she was born from Zeus himself (like Dionysus in his second birth, incidentally, sown into Zeus's thigh) — and ending in her fundamental characteristics: wisdom and courage, two typical features of male Indo-European solar culture. The Apollonian androgyne is an entity in which the female [adj.] is reduced to a minimum and transformed into the male [adj.]. The Cybelean androgyne — Agdistis — is the opposite case. I address this in the first volume of *Noomachy*. In this case, on the contrary, the female [adj.] completely seizes and subjugates the male [adj.]. This male principle is placed inside the female one like a fold, a muscle spasm of the Great Mother. Essentially, this is Dionysus's double, Attis or Adonis. The Great Mother parthenogenetically produces from herself the male alter-ego, which it falls in love with and takes delight in, but which it later castrates and kills, returning to the bottomless darkness of its desperate and insatiable female privation. The Son-Beloved of the Great Mother is a man only externally. Internally he is the Mother herself. The skoptsy and eunuchs are ritual types of this androgyne.

NS: You say that each time a generation of the Great Mother (Titans, Giants) challenges the Olympian gods, they suffer defeat, and you unexpectedly add, "Or is that so only in the Olympian versions of the myth?" This forces one to think. Even more so, it knocks the ground out from under one's feet. Indeed, until now we have known about Titanomachy and Gigantomachy from ancient sources, whose creators were poets and mythographers clearly standing on the side of the gods of Olympus (Hesiod, Homer, Pausanias, Apollodorus, Onomacritus, and others). Neither Xenophanes, nor Democritus, nor Leucippus, nor Epicurus, nor other "priests" of the Great Mother said a word about the battle of Titans and gods (although I should note that Xenophanes did decide to ridicule Titanomachy in his satirical verses). Do you admit the existence of another, "non-Olympian" version of these myths? Not one source has come down to us in which we could see "reversed proportions," i.e. the final victory of the Titans over the gods, but in *Noomachy* you mention the literary works of later periods where a similar finale occurs. I recall that, for instance, Hölderlin's poem "Nature and Art, or Saturn and Jupiter" calls for the "restoration by the Olympian gods of the entire titanic sphere, so that Zeus would give thanks to Kronos and serve him." That is not the only example.

AD: Yes, the stories connected with Prometheus among the Romantics (Keats) also belong here, or the romanticization of Lucifer among the Decadents. The Gigantomachy and Titanomachy of classical antiquity were described by members of orthodox Indo-European culture from the position of two higher functions: priests and warriors. Metaphysical models of the third caste, or even more peripheral elements, indeed suppressed this line, avoiding strict, *belliciste* models, as befits peaceful workers, but the insurrection of the Earth against the Sky, i.e. of producers under the leadership of the god-fighting bourgeois, or revolutionaries against the clergy and aristocracy, is a phenomenon of modernity, and precisely then was the Titanomachy again broadly disseminated in culture, but this time seen through the eyes of the Titans. It is possible that we can find traces of this picture in other civilizations, for instance in the ancient Semitic one, and also among "sea peoples," representatives of the pre-Indo-European matriarchy in the Mediterranean. True, in these cases the scenarios of inverted Titanomachy, described from the position of the Titans, was not fully preserved, and we are forced to reconstruct the topic from indirect data.

NS: What in your opinion is Cybele's main secret? The chthonic double of Dionysus?

AD: Cybele has many secrets. Nietzsche said that a woman must find a depth in her surface. Cybele is extremely banal, but this banality has its own special endless depth. One of Cybele's secrets is infernal parthenogenesis or the simulacrum of divine parthenogenesis. Mother Earth begets Titans, and that is also a secret: from where does she get the solar seed, the eidetic impulse necessary for conception? Or does she operate with a simulacrum of the eidos, with an eidolon? Everything connected with Cybele raises questions. … As for Dionysus's double, that is in fact the main problem of eschatology. Christianity expresses that metaphysical dilemma in the pair Christ-Antichrist. In the second volume of *Noomachy*, "The Logos of Europe," I come to the conclusion that the problematic of Dionysus's double determines the nerve of European philosophy and the culture of modernity, but that concerns not only European civilization. I suspect that Dionysus's chthonic double stands at the center of a few other civilizations also, which makes this problem almost universal, though I reject all universalism, or at least the kind that projects the typological problems of one civilization onto another. So we must raise and study the problem of Dionysus's double very delicately and carefully, without disrupting the inner proportions of each civilization. Nevertheless, I am inclined to think that that is one of the main themes of any civilization, especially the one in which the Logos of Cybele and the Logos of Dionysus predominate.

Dionysus's double appears in the juxtaposition of two zones; the zone of Cybele's influence and the zone of influence of Dionysus proper. The most difficult and most important problems of metaphysics and eschatology are concentrated there.

NS: Do you share the hope of the ancient epopts for the rebirth and coming of a "third Dionysus," the last king?

AD: I am an Orthodox Christian and I experience this eschatological and metaphysical problem as an expectation [*ozhidaniye*, awaiting] of the Second Coming of Christ.

9.

THE EXISTENTIAL
THEORY OF SOCIETY

Implicit Sociology

Alfred Schütz, Husserl's student, applied philosophical phenomenology to the domain of society.[2] As a result of doing so, he developed an original theory that enriched the discipline of sociology. We can do something analogous with Martin Heidegger's philosophy. Neither Heidegger nor Husserl was especially occupied with society and *a fortiori* sociology, but the profundity of their methods and novelty of their perspectives concerning the essential problems of gnoseology and ontology fully permit application to diverse areas of expertise, including those to which they did not give their attention for one reason or another. To do so is entirely in the spirit of Heidegger's own thought, as he asserted that philosophy contains all other sciences in paradigmatic form, *in nuce*. It is a technical question to extract from a full-fledged and original philosophy a spectrum of disciplines implicitly contained in it. On the whole, the construction of the Fourth

---

2   Alfred Schütz, *The Phenomenology of the Social World* (Evanston, IL: Northwestern University Press, 1967).

Political Theory is based in many respects on Heidegger's philosophy and represents precisely the development of implicit content. Since the domain of the political is intimately connected to the domain of the social, an outline of Heideggerian sociology will be extremely useful in the matter of constructing the Fourth Political Theory more generally.

Heidegger almost never uses the term "society" (*Gesellschaft*),[3] but one encounters the term "narod" (*Volk*) in his texts rather often. We will rely primarily on the lecture course from the summer of 1934, *Logic as the Question Concerning The Essence of Language*[4] and the *Black Notebooks*,[5] where Heidegger recalls the "narod" (*Volk*) most often and where he lays the foundations for the further development of his implicit teaching about society.

Volk Als Dasein

First we should consider the central concept of all of Heidegger's philosophy: Dasein. Dasein's peculiarity consists in the fact that it cannot be regarded strictly as either individual human being or as collective, i.e. social [being]. Dasein is primary in relation to both individual and society. Everything that is human originates from Dasein; accordingly, Dasein is pre-individual and pre-social, but at the same time Heidegger's existential analytic brings the most diverse aspects of human thought, action, culture, and habits — i.e. existence — into correlation with Dasein on the whole, so Dasein explains the individual that it includes wholly in itself. There is nothing in the individual human

---

3   And when he does use it, he interprets it in the spirit of Hegel, as an artificial joining of atomized, modern individuals, which does not evoke the least sympathy in him.

4   Martin Heidegger, *Logic as the Question Concerning the Essence of Language* (Albany: SUNY Press, 2009).

5   Martin Heidegger, *Ponderings II–VI: Black Notebooks 1931–1938* (Bloomington: Indiana University Press, 2016), Martin Heidegger, *Ponderings VII–XI: Black Notebooks 1938–1939* (Bloomington: Indiana University Press, 2017).

entity that would not be in Dasein. That is the basis for the existential analytic. Everything that is human is traced to Dasein and finds its sanction [*razresheniye*] in it.

This is explicit with regard to the individual, but we could do exactly the same thing with regard to society. After all, society is purely human. Accordingly, just as with the individual, society is rooted in Dasein and sanctioned [*razreshayetsya*] in it. Like an individual, a society should have existentials, and so we can perfectly well set ourselves the task of an existential analytic of society. Dasein is neither individual nor social (collective), but the individual, on the contrary, leads to Dasein and is contained in it. This is also true of society. Society is also contained in Dasein. It follows that society can be examined from the perspective of Dasein, as Dasein itself.

It is important that Heidegger strictly distinguishes "I" (*ich*) and Selbst. Selbst is the common root of the human and society (narod).

Heidegger says:

> Selbst is not exclusively a determination of the ego, 'I' (*ich*). That is the fundamental error of modernity. Selbst is not determined from the ego, 'I' (*ich*). On the contrary, the Selbst-character is also inherent in 'you [singular],' 'we,' and 'you [plural].' Selbst is mysterious in some new sense. The Selbst-character does not belong exclusively only to 'you,' 'me,' 'us,' but to all equally in a primordial way.[6]

Selbst thus precedes both the singular and the collective, being a common basis for both. So we can very well set ourselves the task of studying the Selbst of society. That entails an entirely peculiar approach to it.

Such a society will be an existential society, and Heidegger uses a special word precisely for society understood in that way: Volk.

Volk is the same as Dasein, but in his philosophy Heidegger is primarily occupied with the delineation of Dasein in the human,

---

6   Heidegger, *Logic as the Question Concerning the Essence of Language.*

philosophy, thought, and culture, and since the problem of the individual as such does not interest him, he constantly moves from the
human to his existential basis, Dasein, most often without specifying
the very structure of this transition. That is why the word Mensch
(human), though used infrequently, is implied in most cases. Each
time it is Mensch als Dasein.

It is entirely legitimate, however, to propose another trajectory to
Dasein: through society. We sometimes see this path in Heidegger,
outlined only very approximately. In these cases he always uses the
word Volk. *Volk als Dasein.*

The Existential Structure of the Volk

Describing the structure of the narod (Volk), Heidegger speaks directly
of a homology with the human.[7] Traditional metaphysics distinguishes
three principles in the human: body, soul, and spirit. We usually do the
same with the narod.

The body of the narod is the space it occupies, and also population,
quantity, demography, production, economy, its wars and peace agree-
ments, and trade and handicrafts.

The soul of the narod is tradition, religion, culture, customs, mo-
res, ethics.

Finally, the spirit of the narod is personified in philosophers, histo-
rians, and rulers who are responsible directly for the fate of the narod
and the state [*gosudarstvo*].

Heidegger discards this classical stratification just as he does the
trichotomous analysis of the human individual. This taxonomy is
a consequence of metaphysics — of Platonic metaphysics, specifi-
cally, but Heidegger calls precisely that metaphysics into question and
strives to break through to the primordial element of thinking. Thus,

_____

7   Heidegger, *Logic as the Question Concerning the Essence of Language.*

he brackets the trichotomous human structure in order, starting the most original of all possible paths, to raise again the question of how we relate to Selbst, of who we are, how we are, and why we are.

The existential analytic, destruction,[8] and transposition into Dasein serve precisely this aim.

As with the individual, the understanding of the narod (Volk) should also not stop at the isolation of three levels — body, spirit, and soul — but should be attained in a new perspective through correlation of the narod with its Selbst, through bringing the narod to Dasein.

In this case, the narod's reliable characteristics will only be its existentials. First of all, these are Sorge (care) and being-toward-death (Sein-zum-Tode).

What we call "the body of the narod" or the economy (Wirtschaft) and production, ceases in this case to be a separate domain, defined by the material factor. Henceforth it is the domain of care [or concern] (Sorge). The narod cares [or is concerned], not because objective circumstances demand it, but in itself, for such is its essence, its Selbst. If we place the narod in the most advantageous circumstances, it will find something to be concerned about. In Heidegger, care is analogous to Husserl's intentional act. Accordingly, a narod's economy, its "body," is nothing but the structure of its intentionality. The economy is intentional, and that is a fundamental conclusion of Heideggerian sociology: it is no accident that the human is involved with labor and production. The production of things with the help of technique is the most vivid form of intentionality. If artificiality of constitution is not apparent when observing natural objects (for those not engaged in

---

8   Destruction or phenomenological destruction as Heidegger understands it in *Being and Time* is the placement of ideas, theories, and statements into their historico-philosophical context, which, according to Heidegger, is the concrete process of the forgetting of being and abandonment of being.

philosophy), in the economic sphere it is explicit. Everything created by man is an intentional object.

To wish that the narod would not create anything artificially, that it would not involve itself in the element of τέχνη (*techne*), is the same as depriving it of intentionality (Sorge), but that is just what Dasein is, which cannot but be concerned.

If this is the "body of the narod" in the existential analytic, then its "soul" and "spirit," that is, culture and philosophy, will not be superstructures on the material basis but will be disclosed as other aspects of that same care, Sorge. After all, the creation of a work of art or philosophical system is nothing other than the result of concern, an intentional act. It is difficult to say where this intentional act is more pure and primordial: on the one hand, among simple people (laborers), the element of care is expressed more immediately and deeply, while poets and thinkers operate with secondary, derivative notions, but on the other hand precisely poets and thinkers stand closer to the risky essence of the creative act. The worker is more existential; Sorge is more vivid and immediate in him. The poet or thinker are inferior to him in this respect, but they relate to the element of death, to nothing, since their creative act is openly dangerous. They are immediately correlated to death. That is what Hegel had in mind in the well-known section on Master and Slave in *The Phenomenology of Spirit*.[9]

Thus, an existential approach requires another — in its turn, existential — structuring of the narod. According to Heidegger, this leads us to distinguish a double horizon. On the whole, the Volk is Dasein, but in a narrow sense, the Volk is Dasein that is given more immediately. Existentials operate in it in full measure and with full power. What is more, the power here is dual: it reflects care (Sorge) more purely — for precisely that reason the majority of people in a given society and culture work, labor, and produce — and at the same time it

---

9   Hegel, *Phenomenology of Spirit*.

covers the gape of death with its powerful torrent. Consequently, the narod (Volk) in the narrow sense, is flight from death. That is why in its usual state the narod is apprehensive (Furcht), but at the same time does not know anxiety [*yzhas*] (Angst).

Another pole or horizon of the narod (Volk) is those Heidegger calls "the single ones" (die Einzelne). This is the instance when Dasein ascends to itself, i.e. to an encounter with being (Sein). Heidegger describes the relation between the narod and the single ones in the *Black Notebooks*:

> The narod: a guarding concealment and primordial manifestation of the legitimation of being. This results from the fertility of thrownness, whose essential con-junction [*vossoyedineniye*] the narod is, and whose great ones remain single ones. The being (essence) of these single ones should be grasped from and within their con-junction [or re-unification] as a narod.[10]

Between the narod and the single one stands the special word Vereinzelung. This word is necessary for Heidegger for pairing the single ones (die Einzelne) and the narod (Volk). The narod is a sort of council [*sobor*] of "single ones," where they can and can no longer remain single ones. The Ver-einzelung is the council as con-junction of single ones, but the choice of Vereinzelung instead of Vereinigung, for instance, shows not only that something is being conjoined, but that the conjoined (the unit, the single one) does not cease being single. Moreover, the narod is not the preceding basis for the single ones and

10 [The Russian text includes the original German passage. Here is Rojcewicz's translation of the original: "*The people:* the guarding and carrying out of the empowerment of being. The empowerment out of the fearfulness of thrownness, whose first essential *individuation* remains precisely the people — and their great *individuals*. The essence of these individuals is to be grasped out of and in the individuation as people."] Martin Heidegger, *Ponderings II-VI: Black Notebooks 1931–1938* (Bloomington: Indiana University Press, 2014): 74 (230) [page 74, entry 230].

their partition: it is already in itself the process of differentiation and integration.

Anyone in the narod can become a single one, and this is marked in it, but only a certain, distinct [person] becomes a single one — i.e. great — placing the accent of his existence on Selbst in its pure guise. What is more, he does not juxtapose himself to the narod and does not even detach himself from it; after all, the narod is Selbst and precisely it, the narod as Selbst, gives the single one his content, his being, and his aim.

Geworfenheit, thrownness, is a Heideggerian existential analogous to the subject. We can say that the narod is a subject, i.e. a horizon of thrownness, and this thrownness grows in the narod in every direction. The single ones are the extreme height of such growth. This height, however, is at the same time depth and return inside the narod, since precisely the narod is the "manifestation of the legitimation of being." The single one reaches being only in the narod and through the narod, since the narod is being, here-being, Dasein.

A DIAGRAM OF THE EXISTENTIAL STRUCTURE OF SOCIETY

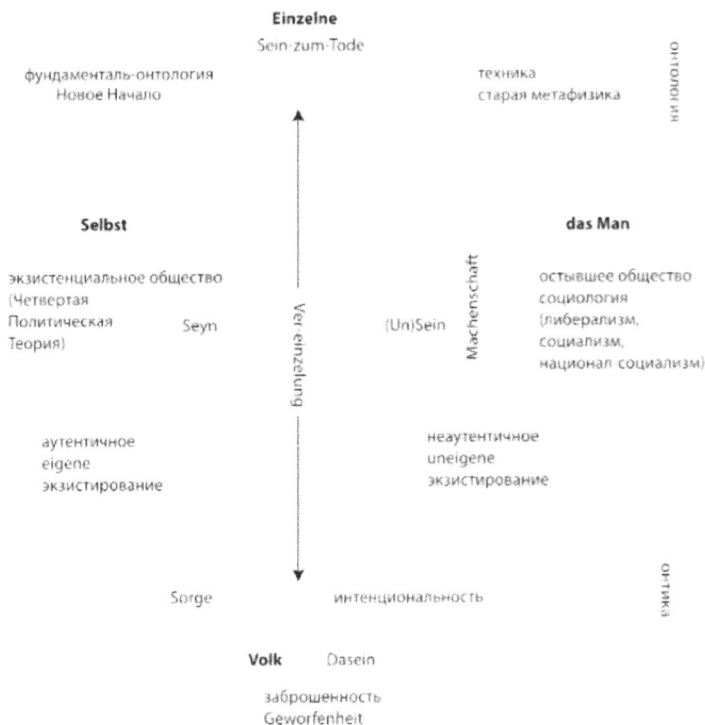

Einzelne

Sein-zum-Tode

фундаменталь-онтология
Новое Начало

техника
старая метафизика

ОНТОЛОГИЯ

Selbst

das Man

экзистенциальное общество
(Четвертая
Политическая
Теория)

Seyn

Vereinzelung

(Un)Sein

Machenschaft

остывшее общество
социология
(либерализм,
социализм,
национал-социализм)

аутентичное
eigene
экзистирование

неаутентичное
uneigene
экзистирование

Sorge

интенциональность

ОНТИКА

Volk   Dasein

заброшенность
Geworfenheit

Схема структуры экзистенциального общества

We see clearly here the unity of the philosophical and sociological conception of Dasein. Heidegger describes the fate of Western Dasein as the gradual cooling-off of the question of being, as the forgetting of being, but the decision (Entscheidung) to remember being (Sein) or to forget it, to think about it or to focus on beings (Seiende), is made always and only by Dasein itself. That is the fundamental thesis of Heideggerian philosophy. That is why Another Beginning of philosophy is possible: Dasein can decide to exist authentically, but it can also decide to exist inauthentically. In the second case rule is given to das Man, who is the "I" or "we" (or "everyone") of inauthentically existing Dasein. In this case, alienated metaphysics and Machenschaft, technique, are affirmed. The single ones in this case become less and less distinguishable from das Man: they are no longer kings and rulers, but "deputies," "commissioners," outspoken "jesters," and "rope walkers" [circus clowns]. That is how political leaders, philosophers, and cultural actors appear, but they are not the ones responsible for that choice. More precisely, deciding to exist inauthentically, they do not act separately and in isolation from Dasein but rather they act thus together with Dasein. Das Man establishes and constitutes a general will. This is an existential act, in the course of which thrown presence turns away from being, that is, from its own essence, its own Selbst.

All this is manifest in the clearest way in sociology also. As the philosophy of modernity represents the systematic forgetting of being, so the political and social teachings of modernity express the same process in their sphere. That is why all types of modern social order, like all forms of political ideology (reducible to the three basic ones of liberalism, communism, and fascism)[11] represent variations of alienated society, where, in the end, das Man, the central figure of Machenschaft, dominates.

At the same time society (in the sense of Gesellschaft), understood as modern society, the society of modernity (in contrast to pre-modern Gemeinschaft, i.e. community) lacks a set of strictly autonomous criteria, although it insists on this in its three basic versions (according to the number of main political theories). All proposed criteria are nothing other than the existentials of Dasein, distorted and alienated, reworked by das Man and the element of Machenschaft.

This begins from the subject itself. In modern philosophy, Descartes announced the subject. In the three modern political theories we are dealing with three narrower interpretations of the subject.

---

11   Alexander Dugin, *The Fourth Way: Introduction to the Fourth Political Theory* (Moscow: Academic Project, 2014).

Liberalism interprets the subject as the individual; communists as the class; fascists as the state [*gosudarstvo*], nation [*natsiya*], or race (national-socialism).

Heidegger shows that the subject is a modern construct [construct of modernity] built on the forgotten Dasein buried beneath it. That is why philosophical destruction begins by dismantling the subject and breaking through to Dasein. If today we project that into society (sociology), we will see that all three subjects of the political theories of modernity (liberalism, communism, fascism) ignore the narod (Volk), which is Dasein. Accordingly, destruction in existential sociology should begin by dismantling the individual, class, and nation-state, to discover at their foundation the true existential foundation that has been subjected to alienation, distortion, and forgetting, i.e. the narod (Volk).

The Project of Authentic Society: The Existential Empire

Here we transition to the projective side of Heidegger, to his notion of how society should be if Dasein chooses in favor of authentic existence, i.e. itself (Selbst). That is the sociological and even political program — Entwurf — of the Fourth Political Theory.

First, everything depends on the decision (Entscheidung), a decision made by Dasein in favor of authentic existence, but the decision is not made by some one person or group of persons, even if they are rulers or are influential, nor by a philosophical school, nor by everyone altogether. There are neither rules nor procedures for the decision at issue. It is something greater. In it, Dasein turns to itself, accomplishes a turning (Kehre), decides on itself, and hazards being. Here Dasein turns directly to its own finitude, i.e. it cooperates with the element of death. Dasein in the whole turns to death, but this turn is sustained only by the separate and rare, the single ones (die Einzelne). The decision manifests itself and makes itself known in them. But they themselves do not make the decision. They are able to carry it out, but not to make it. The narod (Volk) makes the decision, though it cannot carry it out by itself, in the narrow, ontic sense.

Thus, the project of authentic society is adopted synchronously and fully by the narod as Dasein, but it is expressed through the single ones (die Einzelne) who become its bearers. They are the true rulers of the Empire of Another Beginning.

Heidegger writes:

> The metaphysics of Dasein must be deepened and broadened in its inner structure to the metaphysics of the (concrete) historical narod.[12]

That means that the transition from philosophy to sociology (society) and politics is a breakthrough into the sphere of the historical. Dasein's decision acquires its proper scope in precisely the historical, the historial (das Geschichtliche and even more precisely das Seynsgeschichtliche). The society ruled by das Man is clearly anti-historical, ex-historical [i.e. outside of history]. Even if they speak constantly of "history," they understand it as an alienated fate, as τέχνη (techne), as the artificial ground and justification of a completely alienated care, occupying the entire space of the momentary. Such "history" is nothing but a counterfeit (anti-phenomenological) ground for the necessity of labor. The narod becomes truly historical (geschichtliche) only when it chooses authentic existence, but then it encounters its finitude, i.e. risk. This encounter has a name: war, the father of things, according to Heraclitus. The elites of all political formations — states — were formed in that way: they are the rank of warriors and masters, entering into personal relations with death. Philosophers are those among them who are so captivated by death and the finitude of existence that they make death the focal point of

---

12   [The Russian text includes the original German passage.]

their existence [*nalichiya*], striving to penetrate into the depth of being on the very border of nothing. Warriors and philosophers, and also poets, make being historical and fill history with ontological content. In this, the narod becomes full and saturated. Its cares — labors, concerns, inclinations, moods — acquire a basis in being and are brought to the roots. A narod that has acquired a historical dimension becomes a narod of being. It not only exists [*sushchestvuyet*], it henceforth is [*yest'*].

For Heidegger and for the Fourth Political Theory, that is a political and social project.

Heidegger writes in the *Black Notebooks*:

> The most important but most remote goal: the historical greatness of the narod in the realization and formation of the power of being.
> The more proximate goal: the establishment of the narod by itself from the loss of roots and excessive partisanship in the state.
> The most proximate goal: the preliminary organization of the narod-community as the Selbst of the narod.[13]

These stages are especially important if, as in Heidegger's own case, transition to the Fourth Political Theory proceeds or is at least reflected on from within the Third political theory. That is precisely why a near aim is overcoming "excessive partisanship in the state." The state is the name of das Man in the Third political theory (fascism, nationalism). Destruction of the state, as an apparatus, as Machenschaft, is the first theoretical task of the Fourth Political Theory. Without that, the narod

---

13 [The Russian text includes the original German passage. Here is Rojcewicz's translation of the original: "The *proper, but most remote goal*: the historical greatness of the people in the effectuation and configuration of the powers of being. The *more proximate goal*: the *coming to themselves* of the people on the basis of their rootedness and their assuming of their mission through the *state*. The *most proximate goal*: the provisional creation of the community of the people — as the *self* of the people." 100, sections 42–3.]

(Volk) as the "subject" of history, as Dasein, won't be discovered and identified.

In a broader context of the political systems of modernity, we can paraphrase the Heideggerian sequence in the following general way:

1. Awakening of the narod as itself (Selbst);

2. Paving the way through alienated forms of subjectivity imposed by modernity: the individual, class, and state (nation, race), with their parallel (phenomenological) destruction (this depends on the starting point for the realization of the project of the Fourth Political Theory, whether it starts within a liberal, communistic, or nationalistic society);

3. Transition to the horizon of great history (die geschichtliche Grösse des Volkes); the full manifestation of the ontological his-torial as the narod's discovery of its own being.

The Narod and Its God: The Religion of Selbst

The final thing to which we should pay attention as we initially ap-proach existential sociology is the question of religion. For many it can seem the most problematic aspect of Heidegger's philosophy and of the Fourth Political Theory as such.

Heidegger himself understands the problem of gods or God inex-tricably from the narod. In the *Black Notebooks* he cites the words of Shatov from Dostoyevsky's *Demons*:

> *He who has no narod [people] also has no god!*[14]

---

14 In a passage of *The Idiot* Dostoyevsky says through the Prince Myshkin, "He who rejects his native land has also rejected his own god." In this case the ex-pression "native land [*rodnaya zemlya*]" should also be understood existentially. Heidegger regarded earth [*zemlya*] as one of the poles of the fourfold (Geviert), and it is significant that he brought together metaphysically earth (Erde) pre-cisely with the Russian narod and Russ (Russland) as such.

And Heidegger agrees with him fully. The narod and God are inextricably bound. There is no god without the narod. After all, God, who is, creates man, but from an existential perspective, man is Dasein, and consequently the narod (Volk). Creating a reasoning, speaking, thinking principle [*nachalo*], God creates the narod, and without the narod, outside the narod, this principle does not exist. If it doesn't exist, then there is no one to witness God, to praise Him, to glorify Him. That is why thought about God outside thought about the narod, separately from it, will be meaningless: in what language, in what formulas, and in what order would such speech take place?! Theology can ignore the narod, but by itself this won't lead to anything but profound distortions. If religion is living, if it is existential, it must be narodnoy [i.e. of or related to the narod, Volk] in the deepest sense of the word.

Hence, thinking about the project of the narod's awakening, Heidegger writes:

Will we dare once more to have gods and with them the truth of the narod?[15]

God (or gods) is the truth of the narod (die Wahrheit des Volkes), but it is also its being, the being that it itself is, in its inner source, in its identity, in its Selbst. It is not important whether we are dealing with polytheistic or monotheistic versions, whether we assert creation or manifestation.

The relation of the narod to God is deeper than these secondary parameters. The narod is, when it has God. If it decides to exist, it decides to have God and, accordingly, to be had by God, to belong to him.

In the Heideggerian version the concretization of religion is not definitive. Something else is more important: how alive God is, how powerful his being is, and, accordingly, how vivified by him is the

---

15 [The Russian text includes the original German passage.]

narod that creates its historical dimension. There cannot be a narod at all without God, and nothing can be said of any historial in that case, but the presence of cults, institutions, and rites is not yet enough. Religion can also exist in the society of das Man. Then it will be another field of care, i.e. a political, economic, or social thing [*instantsiya*]. In this sort of religion, God dies, and when purely secular political regimes of modernity come (liberalism, communism, fascism), they do not so much "kill" Him as confirm His already accomplished death. Heidegger appeals not to the consequences, but to the causes: faith must be hazarded, decided for. After all, God is the death of man.[16] He embodies in himself that proportion in which the limits of the thinking principle [*nachalo*] are established strictly and ruthlessly. We become mortal only before the face of the Immortal, but we also become persons in that same moment. God creates only that which is, but that is Dasein.

In the Fourth Political Theory, religion is not a contribution of tradition, not simply a rudimentary feature of the past — all the more so since our past is atheistic modernity. In the Fourth Political Theory, the narod decides to have God, and Dasein itself makes this decision, Dasein as the narod (Volk). If in metaphysics, philosophy, and sociology, the Fourth Political Theory is revolutionary (conservative-revolutionary), in the sphere of religion it must also be. Thus, the faith of the narod awakened to history is hazarded faith in the Living God, in the Selbst of God, in God as an antithesis of his institutionalized simulacrum, the Grand Inquisitor. Dostoyevsky's Grand Inquisitor is the title that das Man carries in the sphere of religion. The religion of the narod will be living and authentic only if it will be the religion of Selbst.

---

16 In Heraclitus' 62ⁿᵈ fragment, we read: ἀθάνατοι θνητοί, θνητοὶ ἀθάνατοι, ζῶντες τὸν ἐκείνων θάνατον, τὸν δὲ ἐκείνων βίον τεθνεῶτες. Mortals are immortal, immortals are mortal; the gods live by the death of persons [*lyudi*], persons [*lyudi*] die by the life of the gods.

10.

THINKING CHAOS AND THE OTHER BEGINNING OF PHILOSOPHY

Chaos did not make it into the context of Greek philosophy. Greek philosophy was developed exclusively as the philosophy of Logos, and we are so accustomed to that state of affairs that we — probably justly from a historical perspective — identify philosophy with the Logos. We do not know another philosophy, and in principle, if we believe, firstly, Friedrich Nietzsche and Martin Heidegger, and then also contemporary postmodern philosophy, we will have to acknowledge that this philosophy, discovered by the Greeks, and built around the Logos, has today fully exhausted its content. It was embodied in technē, in the subject-object distinction, and proved sound for two or three centuries, until the final setting chord of Western European philosophy. Today we stand at the limit or end of this philosophy of Logos.

From here we can grasp at a glance the entire process of development of logocentric philosophy. It began with Heraclitus and the pre-Socratics, reached its apogee in Platonism and Socrates, developed rapidly in Greco-Latin patristics, and later in Scholasticism and the Neo-Platonism of the Renaissance, finally turning into modernity altogether, with Descartes and his subject-object distinction through to the last, self-reflexive stage, ending with Nietzsche. According to Heidegger, Nietzsche put an end to Western European philosophy. Thus, before us is a complete account [or story, *rasskaz*] of logocentric culture, with a beginning, apogee, and denouement. The Logos from birth to death. Who, then, was Heidegger?

On one hand, Heidegger closes this process of Western philosophy for good and gives it its final seal; on the other hand, he lays the potential foundations for something new. The end of philosophy is indisputable; the question about "another beginning," *die andere Anfang* is open.

Western European philosophy, being logocentric, has exhausted its potential. However, we should raise a question here: what role did *Chaos* play in this logocentric philosophy? It was discarded from the beginning, bracketed, crossed out, because Logos is based on the exclusion of Chaos, on the affirmation of a strict alternative to it. What is the fundamental difference between Logos and Chaos? Logos is exclusivity, Logos is division, Logos is a clear-cut notion of this and the other, and it is no accident that Logos was formalized in Aristotle's logic, in its basic laws: the law of identity, the law of contradiction, and the law of the excluded middle. It is necessary to emphasize that contemporary modern and postmodern studies show, correctly, that the logocentric understanding of the world is masculinoid, i.e. exclusively male and exclusivist.[17] Men regard the world and order in just that way, as disconnected. Logos is the male, hierarchic principle; it emptied itself in Western European philosophy, reached its highest point, and ... collapsed, was overthrown, and dissipated. Today, the "great man," the "cosmic man," has disintegrated into fragments. He

---

17 See the problematic of the diurnal in Durand's regimes of the imagination. Alexander Dugin, *Sociology of the Imagination* (Moscow: Academic Project, 2010).

collapsed, and together with him, his philosophy, since Logos and the male principle are essentially the same thing, hence the competence of the postmodern, critical term phallo-logocentrism. All Western European philosophy was built on the male principle from beginning to end. The end is here. We are living through it. The Logos is exhausted, so it remains either to slip compliantly into the night or to search for new paths.

Here it must be said at once that the Chaos dealt with by modern science, modern physics, and chaos theory, in fact, represents structures of order, though more complex forms of it. This Chaos is nothing other than complex systems; not at all an alternative to order as such, but only an extravagant, baroque version of a complicated, distorted, and to a significant extent perverted *order* (relevant here are the ideas of the postmodernist Gilles Deleuze, set forth by him in the essay *The Fold: Leibniz and the Baroque*). What the representatives of science, and, in part, culture, call "chaos" today is a condition of the post-logical world, which is still nevertheless found on this side of Logos, within its orbits, though on its periphery, and in its outermost district. René Guénon gave a very precise name to this state of affairs, calling it *la confusion.*

The understanding of "chaos" prevalent in contemporary science does not at all correspond to Greek Chaos as something primordial, organic, and spontaneous, but is rather a product of the collapse of logocentric philosophy and the logocentric culture based on it. What we are dealing with today with the so-called "chaos" is a product of the collapse of Logos, the dissipation of it, and its dispersion into separate fragments. That is precisely why scientists researching "chaos" find in it the residual, or extravagant, eccentric structures of Logos. These structures lend themselves to studying and counting only in more complex procedures with the help of a specific apparatus adapted to the calculation and description of bifurcational processes, non-integrable equations (Prigogine), and fractals (Mandelbrot). "Chaos" theory studies processes that are highly dependent on initial conditions. "Chaos" is defined commonly as a dynamic system with the following features: sensitivity to initial conditions, the property of topological mixing, and density of periodic orbits.[18]

This "chaos" isn't the Greek Chaos at all, but the product of the dispersion and collapse of Logos. We still have not left the limits of the Logos: the Chaos that contemporary science deals with is enclosed within Logos, splashing around in its inner expanses, although in the furthest orbit. It lies at the greatest distance from the vertical, ordering, and logocentric axis, at the outer regions of the Platonic, speculative cosmos, and in the world of the Titans.[19] Thus, strictly speaking, we should call this reality "a very distant copy," which has almost entirely lost its connection with the original. This is not at all "chaos." The term "confusion" (Guénon's *la confusion*) or the postmodern notion of a "simulacrum" interpreted by Baudrillard as "copy without an original" fits best here. This inner-logical zone, though maximally remote from the center, has nothing in common with the primordial Greek model of Chaos, which, according to myth, precedes Logos, or order, i.e. cosmos. True Chaos is pre-logical and pre-ontological. The "confusion" or "chaos" of contemporary science is post-cosmic, and although practically no being remains in it, it nevertheless is there, which means that it is to a certain extent ontological. Fully pertinent here is Zeno's paradox about swift-footed Achilles and the tortoise. However much "confusion" might strive to rid itself of ontology, it is not able to do so; the limit of x, when x approaches zero, will never be equal to zero, but will only constantly approximate zero. It will always remain at an

---

18   Martin Gutzwiller, *Chaos in Classical and Quantum Mechanics* (New York: Springer-Verlag, 1990).

19   Proclus, *Commentaire sur le Timee* (Par A. J. Festugiere. t. I. P.: Vrin, 1966).

ever decreasing, but nevertheless infinitely large (though also infinitely small!), distance from it.[20]

In studying "chaos" (Gilles Deleuze describes this as the means of co-existence of impossible monads; he calls such "monads" "nomads"),[21] contemporary science studies an inner-logical, post-logical, dissipative order, and not at all an alternative to order, as the nihilistically oriented postmodernists had hoped.

Here it is important to pay attention to the concept of "nothing." Logos gathers everything into itself and ascribes to everything the property of self-identity in connection with itself, i.e. with Logos. Logos is everything, and it gathers everything into itself except for what it is not; but what it is not is nothing. Logos excludes everything that it does not include, but since it includes everything, only nothing remains outside it, but it treats this nothing harshly. In the words of Parmenides, non-being is not. Nothing encircles order, serving as its boundary, but since we are looking at nothing through the eyes of Logos, this boundary cannot be reached. However much we might strive toward nothing, whatever nihilism we might cultivate, we remain within the limits of something, but not nothing. We remain within order, under the hegemony of Logos. Although this hegemony weakens at the remote periphery, it never disappears entirely. That is why, on the path of liberation from power and domination, moderns, and after them, postmoderns, discover after God and traditional society the figure of the "despot" in society as such, then in reason, then in the human himself, then in structures, then language, and finally context (post-structuralism), etc. The fact that non-being is not makes being insuperable for those to whom its weight is a burden. All evocations of "chaos" or appeals to "nomadic," impossible monads, cannot produce the desired result: a final and irreversible uprooting of "the

---

20 René Guénon, *Les principes du calcul infinitésimal* (Paris, Gallimard, 1946).

21 Deleuze, *The Fold*.

will to power," which is the main aim of the emancipatory program of the Enlightenment. It will not succeed and can never succeed by definition.

Those who understand the profound crisis of modernity (Martin Heidegger in particular) turn to the roots of the West, to the Greek matrix from which philosophy was born. Heidegger thoroughly investigates the birth of Logos and monitors its fate through to the reign of technique, *Machenschaft*. To describe this [process], he introduces the concept "*Gestell*," which he uses to sum up the self-referential theory of truth — from Plato (and even Heraclitus) to the mechanical commercial-material civilization of extreme contemporary decadence (which is planetary, but still Western-centric). Taking in the history of philosophy at a glance, which is history as such, from beginning to end, Heidegger discovers that it ended so wrongly precisely because it began so wrongly. As an alternative he outlines the project of "another Beginning."[22]

After describing the first Beginning of philosophy, which led first to the Logos, and ultimately to the dissipative post-logical (and post-masculine) ontology in which we are living, Heidegger identifies it as the consequence of a fundamental mistake made in the first stages of Western European philosophy. In his perspective, the history of Western European philosophy, culture, and religion, is the result of a small initial error in metaphysical contemplation. Two and a half thousand years of human history, according to Heidegger, were in vain, because in the very beginning, somewhere in the zone of the initial formulations of the status of Logos, a mistake was inadvertently made. This, Heidegger thinks, it is necessary to become aware of, first, and, second, to overcome. That is how his conception of two Beginnings in philosophy is formed. The first Beginning of philosophy began, took

---

22 Alexander Dugin, *Martin Heidegger: The Philosophy of Another Beginning* (Washington Summit, 2014).

shape, came into its own, blossomed, and then degraded, and has now come to naught (let's remember contemporary nihilism, discovered by Nietzsche, and thoroughly analyzed by Heidegger). *Another Beginning* might have been found in the origins of philosophy, but this did not happen and the result is evident: Logos and its deprivation. In any case, it must be emphasized and begun now, when everything is clear. This beginning, however, begins only if everything becomes truly clear. It became clear to Heidegger — for the rest, [there was] a "delay" and [things are] apparently "not yet" [clear], *noch nicht*, the eternal "not yet." This other beginning is *die andere Anfang*.

If we carefully examine what Heidegger means by "another Beginning," an alternative possible Beginning that hasn't yet taken place or occurred, and if we follow the line of the grandiose deconstruction of Logos he undertook, we shall be able to take in at a glance all Western European philosophy, culture, and history, including [the] religious [aspects], since religion is nothing other than the development of logical constructions (which is why Heidegger talks of "theology" — Christian religion, like Islamic kalam and theological Judaism, is based on Logos; in principle we do not have any monotheistic religions besides the religions of Logos). The logocentrism of religions is extremely important to understand: it shows that it is useless to appeal to religion in search of an alternative to or defense against the failure of Logos: the crisis of contemporary religions is a crisis of Logos; when Logos fails, its entire vertical topos [*topika*] falls with all its variations, including theological ones. This is interconnected: monotheism loses its fascination, since the attraction of Logos weakens, and vice versa. Religions without Logos cease to be themselves, but even in this case, Logos will be present in them, as phantom pain, as "confusion," and as the bustle of desemantised fragments (as we see around us today in the doubtful phenomenon of the so-called "religious awakening," which unambiguously gives us simulacrum and parody).

This is why Heidegger proposed to look for an exit rather differently: on the one hand, in the very Beginning, in the sources of Greek philosophy, even at the threshold of that Beginning, and on the other hand, beyond the limits of our world, thereby uniting the problematic of the moment of origin of philosophy, its dwelling in an embryonic, ante-natal state, with the problematic of the moment of its final agony and death. Before Heraclitus, philosophy was in the womb, Logos "swam" in maternal waters, in the matrix. Today, Logos lies in the tomb. Tomb and womb on one hand have antithetical meanings: death in the former, birth in the latter; but at the same time we know that in the collective unconscious they are synonyms, reciprocal systems. Figuratively, we can say that in both cases it is night, darkness, existence without distinction, the erasing of borders, and nocturne,[23] the more so since many initiatory rituals are connected with immersion in a tomb as the beginning of resurrection, i.e. *another*, second birth. Such is the rite of Orthodox baptism: water in Orthodox baptism symbolizes the earth, tomb, and death. The complete triple submersion of the baptized in the font is a symbol of Christ's three days in the tomb. This submersion into the earth, the tomb, "entombment to Christ," is a pledge for a new birth.

Thus, if in the first beginning of Greek philosophy, Logos was born through the rejection of Chaos as the principle of division, hierarchy, and exclusion, and order was placed exclusively in the center of the All, then, essentially, the male principle was elevated into the absolute. If all this began and ended with what we have in the contemporary world, then, accordingly, following Heidegger, we must trace what was overlooked. We must find what the mistake was in the first impulse that gave the start to the unfolding of logocentric civilization. Heidegger develops his vision in the summarizing and exceedingly complex work *Beitrage zur Philosophie*, with which I encourage everyone to

23 Alexander Dugin, *Sociology of the Imagination*.

familiarize themselves (the work is not translated and that, I would say, is wonderful: it cannot be translated. There are some things that are not only difficult to translate, but criminal to translate. One must learn the language to understand).[24] "Another beginning" is discussed there directly and we find a short and relatively "easy" synopsis of these ideas in *Geschichte des Seyns* as well.[25]

Heidegger proposes thinking *radically different* than is usual in existing philosophical, or philosophico-religious thought, but how is it possible to philosophize differently? How can there be "another Beginning" of philosophy? If we carefully examine the birth of Greek philosophy, we will see one fundamental thing: *philosophy is born together with exclusion*, and what is more, the first to be excluded is Chaos. Chaos is not a philosophical concept and never was one, but it enters philosophy exclusively through its intermediary, through its substitute in the figure of *Khôra*, the Platonic "space" in the *Timaeus*, or as the later "matter" (*hyle*) of Aristotle. However, the perspective on *Khôra* in the *Timaeus* and on matter in Aristotle is already the perspective of Logos,[26] but everything said by Logos about that which it has already excluded in the course of its accession is like "political propaganda" or a "news release." That which Logos tells us about matter is entirely a constructivist *Wille zur Macht*, "will to power," the deployment of a biased and aggressive strategy of male domination, the establishment of hierarchical hegemony, the projection of wishful thinking, and a self-fulfilling prophecy. From the very beginning of philosophy, "the tail wags the dog."

24 Heidegger M., *Beiträge zur Philosophie* (Frankfurt am Main: Vittorio Klostermann, 2003). [Martin Heidegger, *Contributions to Philosophy (of the Event)* (Bloomington: Indiana University Press, 2012).]

25 Heidegger M., *Geschichte des Seyns* (Frankfurt am Main: Vittorio Klostermann, 1998). [Martin Heidegger *The History of Beyng* (Bloomington: Indiana University Press, 2015).]

26 Alexander Dugin, *Martin Heidegger: The Possibility of Russian Philosophy.*

Philosophy tries to impose on us what is advantageous to itself. Here lies the source of male cunning, his striving to absolutize himself, and, accordingly, to exclude the female principle [beginning], and "*the other*" principle [or: another beginning]. Behind this, we can discern a complete and total *lack of understanding of the woman*. Hence the ascription to woman of properties she does not in fact possess. Thus the male formats under himself that which he excludes from the intellectual process. Logos refuses *Khôra* the quality of intelligibility, but it doesn't understand it only because it doesn't want to. It prefers to deal with representations instead. A man thinks that the sole means to get to know a woman is to hide her in inner repose, to deprive her of her public, social dimension, and then to banish her altogether, destroying her traces through the torment of lonely male askesis. Hence, Logos's opinion about Chaos is obvious falsity. It is violence, subjection, hegemony, and the exclusion of Chaos as other. Since Logos is everything, Chaos becomes *nothing*.[27]

If we want to understand the possibility of "another Beginning" of philosophy, we must come to the birth of Logos and fasten upon this transition across the border, discerning the details and semantics of this *rite du passage*. How is it that Logos got out, and separated itself, and who allowed it to issue its exclusive decrees regarding Chaos? Most interestingly, if we sense the inadequacy of dissipative logical and post-logical structures, we must become aware that it is necessary to turn to Logos anew, since Logos itself produced, by its exclusivity, all the preconditions of this dissipation. We cannot simply pick up and return to Platonism: there is no path backward [*obratnogo puti*]. Logos only moves in one direction: it splinters and splinters (and splinters and splinters...).[28] Gilbert Durand calls this logic the regime of the

---

27 Ibid.

28 On "diaresis" and the regime of the "diurne," which are the distinctive signs of the work of Logos, see Alexander Dugin, *Sociology of the Imagination*.

"diurne": it won't stop until it reduces everything to a crumb.[29] This schizomorphe[30] leads directly to Deleuze and Guattari's "schizomass" concept.[31] It is wonderfully depicted in the films of Takashi Miike, for instance in *Ichi the Killer* or *Izo*. In *Izo*, having started a battle against the world, a mad samurai does not stop until he cuts into pieces absolutely everything that falls into his hands. Izo is the Logos.

Logos will not help us. If we are not pleased by the way the contemporary, post-logical world is ordered, like it or not, we must turn to Chaos. We have no other alternative: we must step fundamentally back to the first Beginning of Greek culture in order to take at least the slightest step forward, truly forward, and not along the infinite arc of the world eternally ending without ever coming to an end ("not-yet"). If we fail to do so, we fall into the eternal dead-end of the endless return of dissipative structure-confusions. The choice: either contemporary post-logical Chaos of confusions, or going beyond them, a way beyond them that can only be found in Chaos, which precedes Logos and is located radically beyond its limit, beyond the line of its peripheral agony.

Chaos can and must be regarded as *inclusive order*, as order based on a contrary principle to Logos, i.e. a principle of inclusion, inclusiveness. That is why it is very important to understand what *inclusiveness* means. Once we understand that, we will learn whether it is possible at all to build the philosophy of Chaos, the philosophy of "another beginning."

It won't work for us to view Chaos as logocentric models view it. There is nothing logical, exclusive, or masculine in Chaos (no *Wille Zur Macht*), so for Logos and Onto-Logos it becomes the *ouk on* (Greek: pure non-being), the French *rien*, the Spanish *nada*. Precisely

29 Durand G., *Les Structures anthropologiques de l'imaginaire* (Paris: P.U.F., 1960).

30 Ibid.

31 Gilles Deleuze, Félix Guattari, *Anti-Oedipus: Capitalism and Schizophrenia* (London: Continuum, 2003).

the *ouk on,* as Greeks called non-being, can produce something from itself ("pregnant non-being"). Since Logos sees nothing but itself, then by a principle of Aristotelian logic there is *nothing* we can oppose to it: either A is equal to A and we are within logical boundaries, or A is not equal to A and we are beyond those boundaries, in nothing. According to Aristotle, the latter means that A just does not exist; the A that would not be equal to A does not exist, in contrast, for example, to the philosophy of the Japanese Kitaro Nishida, who, despite Aristotle, elaborated a special logical place, "basho," based on Zen Buddhist models of thought.

Outside of Logos and its hypnotic suggestions, however, Chaos can full well be conceptualized — as the principle of absolute inclusion or of inclusive philosophy. Why is this possible? Because if we disregard the political propaganda of the Logos, under which we have lived for two and a half millennia, we will be able to see Chaos as it presents *itself,* and not as it is presented by Logos. Chaos reveals itself as that which is inclusive and carries in itself *all* possibilities, including the possibility of exclusion, right up to the exclusion of itself. Indeed, in Chaos there is Logos, and [the Logos is] precisely as it thinks *itself.* Like an embryo in the womb of a woman, it is and will be born, without fail. It will be torn away. It will mature and leave, but behind the scenes something more important will remain, the one that enables it to live, produces, nurtures, and feeds it.

Logos can be thought of as a *fish* swimming in the waters of Chaos. Without this water, discarded on the surface, a fish will die. That, in effect, is how the structures of Logos have "died." We are dealing only with its dissipative vestiges, the bones of the fish discarded on the shore, and it is no accident that many are speaking about the symbolism of the new waters of Aquarius, without which the old fish could not live.

The philosophy of Chaos is possible because, being all-inclusive and all-embracing, Chaos precedes any exclusion, containing this exclusion in itself, but only relating to it, and to itself, *differently* than exclusion, i.e. Logos, relates to Chaos and to itself. We only know one perspective on Chaos, the philosophical perspective from the position of Logos, but if we want to look at Logos from the perspective of Chaos, we are told that it is impossible, since we have become accustomed to looking *only* from the perspective of Logos. It is thought that only Logos has sight, while Chaos is blind. No, this is not right; Chaos has a thousand eyes, it is "panoptic." Chaos sees itself as that which contains Logos in itself; hence, Logos is within Chaos and can be in it always, but containing Logos in itself, Chaos contains it entirely differently than the Logos contains itself. Logos rejects that it is contained in anything, even itself, and accordingly pushes Chaos outside the limits, equating it to nothing, disclaiming it. Thus, becoming aware of itself as something distinct from the waters surrounding it, the fish concludes that it no longer needs the water and throws itself on the shore. However often one might throw this stupid fish back, it will repeat its leap over and over again. This insane fish was called Aristotle.

Water, however, is the beginning of everything. It contains the root of other elements and other entities. It carries in itself that which it is and that which it is not. It includes in itself that which recognizes this fact, and that which does not.

From the foregoing we can draw the following conclusions: first, the philosophy of Chaos is possible; secondly, it is not possible to save Logos through Logos; Logos can be saved only through the correct appeal to Chaos.

Chaos is not simply not "old," it is always "new," because eternity is always new; the eternity (*l'éternité*) that Rimbaud found (*a retrouvé*), *c'est la mer allée avec le soleil*. Note, *la mer*. Chaos is the newest, freshest, and most fashionable, the very latest from this season's collection (*Il faut être absolument moderne. Point de cantiques: tenir le pas gagné*). Precisely because it is absolutely eternal: time becomes antiquated very quickly, yesterday's time looks archaic (there is nothing older than "news" from last month's newspaper); only eternity is always new. That is why the disclosure of Chaos does not mean going deep into history, into structures that seem overcome by historical time; no, it is an encounter with the eternally young. Chaos was not sometime before, back then. Chaos is here and now. Chaos is not that which was, as Logos propagandizes it. Chaos is that which is, and Chaos is *that which will be.*

In conclusion, let us return again to Heidegger. It is only possible to break through to the truth of being (*Wahrheit des Seyns*) at two moments of history: at the Beginning, when philosophy is just being born, and at the End, when the disappearance and liquidation of philosophy is occurring. Of course, separate individuals could accomplish this breakthrough at other stages, too, but they could do this or content themselves with something else — they lived in the magic of Logos, warming themselves in the rays of the solar seed.

Today this is the only thing left for us; everything else has been exhausted, and to be contented by dissolution in the world eternally ending and never coming to an end, in the "not-yet," is the lot of nobodies [*nichtozhestv*]. Moreover, it is easier to do so today than ever before. We live together in an astonishing time, when the once completely unexpected possibility of getting to know Chaos directly is opening before us. The experience is not for weak souls. After all, our task is the construction of the philosophy of Chaos.

OTHER BOOKS PUBLISHED BY ARKTOS

SRI DHARMA PRAVARTAKA ACHARYA — *The Dharma Manifesto*

JOAKIM ANDERSEN — *Rising from the Ruins*

WINSTON C. BANKS — *Excessive Immigration*

ALAIN DE BENOIST — *Beyond Human Rights*
Carl Schmitt Today
The Ideology of Sameness
The Indo-Europeans
Manifesto for a European Renaissance
On the Brink of the Abyss
The Problem of Democracy
Runes and the Origins of Writing
View from the Right (vol. 1–3)

ARMAND BERGER — *Tolkien, Europe, and Tradition*

ARTHUR MOELLER VAN DEN BRUCK — *Germany's Third Empire*

MATT BATTAGLIOLI — *The Consequences of Equality*

KERRY BOLTON — *The Perversion of Normality*
Revolution from Above
Yockey: A Fascist Odyssey

ISAC BOMAN — *Money Power*

CHARLES WILLIAM DAILEY — *The Serpent Symbol in Tradition*

RICARDO DUCHESNE — *Faustian Man in a Multicultural Age*

ALEXANDER DUGIN — *Ethnos and Society*
Ethnosociology
Eurasian Mission
The Fourth Political Theory
The Great Awakening vs the Great Reset
Last War of the World-Island
Political Platonism
Putin vs Putin
The Rise of the Fourth Political Theory
The Theory of a Multipolar World

EDWARD DUTTON — *Race Differences in Ethnocentrism*

MARK DYAL — *Hated and Proud*

CLARE ELLIS — *The Blackening of Europe*

KOENRAAD ELST — *Return of the Swastika*

JULIUS EVOLA — *The Bow and the Club*
Fascism Viewed from the Right
A Handbook for Right-Wing Youth
Metaphysics of Power
Metaphysics of War
The Myth of the Blood
Notes on the Third Reich
Pagan Imperialism
Recognitions
A Traditionalist Confronts Fascism

GUILLAUME FAYE — *Archeofuturism*

OTHER BOOKS PUBLISHED BY ARKTOS

	Archeofuturism 2.0
	The Colonisation of Europe
	Convergence of Catastrophes
	Ethnic Apocalypse
	A Global Coup
	Prelude to War
	Sex and Deviance
	Understanding Islam
	Why We Fight
DANIEL S. FORREST	*Suprahumanism*
ANDREW FRASER	*Dissident Dispatches*
	Reinventing Aristocracy in the Age of Woke Capital
	The WASP Question
GÉNÉRATION IDENTITAIRE	*We are Generation Identity*
PETER GOODCHILD	*The Taxi Driver from Baghdad*
	The Western Path
PAUL GOTTFRIED	*War and Democracy*
PETR HAMPL	*Breached Enclosure*
PORUS HOMI HAVEWALA	*The Saga of the Aryan Race*
LARS HOLGER HOLM	*Hiding in Broad Daylight*
	Homo Maximus
	Incidents of Travel in Latin America
	The Owls of Afrasiab
RICHARD HOUCK	*Liberalism Unmasked*
A. J. ILLINGWORTH	*Political Justice*
ALEXANDER JACOB	*De Naturae Natura*
JASON REZA JORJANI	*Artemis Unveiled*
	Closer Encounters
	Faustian Futurist
	Iranian Leviathan
	Lovers of Sophia
	Novel Folklore
	Prometheism
	Promethean Pirate
	Prometheus and Atlas
	Uber Man
	World State of Emergency
HENRIK JONASSON	*Sigmund*
EDGAR JULIUS JUNG	*The Significance of the German Revolution*
RUUBEN KAALEP & AUGUST MEISTER	*Rebirth of Europe*
RODERICK KAINE	*Smart and SeXy*
PETER KING	*Here and Now*
	Keeping Things Close
	On Modern Manners

OTHER BOOKS PUBLISHED BY ARKTOS

JAMES KIRKPATRICK	*Conservatism Inc.*
LUDWIG KLAGES	*The Biocentric Worldview*
	Cosmogonic Reflections
	The Science of Character
ANDREW KORYBKO	*Hybrid Wars*
PIERRE KREBS	*Guillaume Faye: Truths & Tributes*
	Fighting for the Essence
JULIEN LANGELLA	*Catholic and Identitarian*
JOHN BRUCE LEONARD	*The New Prometheans*
STEPHEN PAX LEONARD	*The Ideology of Failure*
	Travels in Cultural Nihilism
WILLIAM S. LIND	*Reforging Excalibur*
	Retroculture
PENTTI LINKOLA	*Can Life Prevail?*
H. P. LOVECRAFT	*The Conservative*
NORMAN LOWELL	*Imperium Europa*
RICHARD LYNN	*Sex Differences in Intelligence*
JOHN MACLUGASH	*The Return of the Solar King*
CHARLES MAURRAS	*The Future of the Intelligentsia &*
	For a French Awakening
JOHN HARMON MCELROY	*Agitprop in America*
MICHAEL O'MEARA	*Guillaume Faye and the Battle of Europe*
	New Culture, New Right
MICHAEL MILLERMAN	*Beginning with Heidegger*
MAURICE MURET	*The Greatness of Elites*
BRIAN ANSE PATRICK	*The NRA and the Media*
	Rise of the Anti-Media
	The Ten Commandments of Propaganda
	Zombology
TITO PERDUE	*The Bent Pyramid*
	Journey to a Location
	Lee
	Morning Crafts
	Philip
	The Sweet-Scented Manuscript
	William's House (vol. 1–4)
JOHN K. PRESS	*The True West vs the Zombie Apocalypse*
RAIDO	*A Handbook of Traditional Living* (vol. 1–2)
CLAIRE RAE RANDALL	*The War on Gender*
STEVEN J. ROSEN	*The Agni and the Ecstasy*
	The Jedi in the Lotus
NICHOLAS ROONEY	*Talking to the Wolf*
RICHARD RUDGLEY	*Barbarians*
	Essential Substances
	Wildest Dreams

OTHER BOOKS PUBLISHED BY ARKTOS

ERNST VON SALOMON	*It Cannot Be Stormed*
	The Outlaws
WERNER SOMBART	*Traders and Heroes*
PIERO SAN GIORGIO	*CBRN*
	Giuseppe
	Survive the Economic Collapse
SRI SRI RAVI SHANKAR	*Celebrating Silence*
	Know Your Child
	Management Mantras
	Patanjali Yoga Sutras
	Secrets of Relationships
GEORGE T. SHAW (ED.)	*A Fair Hearing*
FENEK SOLÈRE	*Kraal*
	Reconquista
OSWALD SPENGLER	*The Decline of the West*
	Man and Technics
RICHARD STOREY	*The Uniqueness of Western Law*
TOMISLAV SUNIC	*Against Democracy and Equality*
	Homo Americanus
	Postmortem Report
	Titans are in Town
ASKR SVARTE	*Gods in the Abyss*
HANS-JÜRGEN SYBERBERG	*On the Fortunes and Misfortunes of Art in Post-War Germany*
ABIR TAHA	*Defining Terrorism*
	The Epic of Arya (2nd ed.)
	Nietzsche's Coming God, or the Redemption of the Divine
	Verses of Light
JEAN THIRIART	*Europe: An Empire of 400 Million*
BAL GANGADHAR TILAK	*The Arctic Home in the Vedas*
DOMINIQUE VENNER	*For a Positive Critique*
	The Shock of History
HANS VOGEL	*How Europe Became American*
MARKUS WILLINGER	*A Europe of Nations*
	Generation Identity
ALEXANDER WOLFHEZE	*Alba Rosa*
	Rupes Nigra

www.ingramcontent.com/pod-product-compliance
Lightning Source LLC
Chambersburg PA
CBHW031139090426
42738CB00008B/1145